I LIKE IT LIKE THAT

I LIKE IT LIKE THAT

True Stories of Gay Male Desire

edited by
Richard Labonté *&* Lawrence Schimel

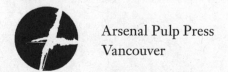

Arsenal Pulp Press
Vancouver

ARSENAL PULP PRESS
Suite 200, 341 Water Street
Vancouver, BC
Canada V6B 1B8
arsenalpulp.com

The publisher gratefully acknowledges the support of the Canada Council for the Arts and the British Columbia Arts Council for its publishing program, and the Government of Canada through the Book Publishing Industry Development Program and the Government of British Columbia through the Book Publishing Tax Credit Program for its publishing activities.

Book design by Shyla Seller
Editing by Susan Safyan
Cover photograph by Noz

Printed and bound in Canada on recycled paper

"Army of Ugly" © 2009 by Daniel Allen Cox. First published in *Capital Xtra!*, Jan. 21, 2009; reprinted with the author's permission.

"The Signal is Jammed: A Confession" © 2009 by Mark Ambrose Harris. An earlier, shorter version was first published as "Electric Blue Aural Body" in *Lickety Split*, Nov. 2008; reprinted with the author's permission.

"A Walk around Eros" © 2006 by Tim Miller. First appeared in *1001 Beds: Performances, Essays, and Travels*, University of Wisconsin Press; reprinted with the author's permission.

"Something About Muscle" © 2003 by Andy Quan. First appeared in *Best Gay Erotica 2003*, Cleis Press; reprinted with the author's permission.

Library and Archives Canada Cataloguing in Publication

          I like it like that : true stories of gay male desire / edited by Richard Labonté and Lawrence Schimel.

ISBN 978-1-55152-259-3

          1. Gay men--Sexual behavior. I. Labonté, Richard, 1949- II. Schimel, Lawrence

PN6120.95.H724I2 2009   306.77086'642   C2009-903729-7

Contents

Introduction: Reflections on What We Like

Richard Labonté and Lawrence Schimel

I Like It Like That is an anthology about gay sexual desire in many, though by no means all, of its forms. We offer a snapshot of the erotic diversity within our homosexual experiences, although these many different voices are no more than the tip of the iceberg—we all have our own particular hot spots.

What turns us on can run the gamut from something ineffable and almost indefinable (the way someone moves, evoking a memory of someone else) to something concrete and quite specific (being blindfolded, pissed on, and fucked by a crowd of anonymous men). Our contributors reach into their sexual memories to tell true tales about personal erotic spaces—these aren't stories drawn from the mainstream porn imagery that by default dominates our cultural (and therefore personal) references. These writers relate what has turned them on in their lives—and why. Their tales are hot, but also smart. They offer passion, but also philosophy. They contain both the urgency of desire and reflections on desire—some accounts dwell on the physical side of sex, some explore a philosophy of the erotic.

Sexual imagery for mass consumption is often extremely codified. We're not going to list here which personal essays are about which specific subjects; the point of this anthology is not to match your fetish interests to a particular essay, but to create a space for discussion of and reflection on what tempts and tickles our libidos, and why.

Which is not to say that there won't be any overlap between your own hot buttons and the contents of these essays. A lot depends on who you are and what you like. It's probable that some of our authors are turned on by what turns you on—tender touch, a wrestling ring, leather and ropes, a jock's Jockeys—while others may get their kicks from situations or objects that leave you feeling cold or even repulsed.

Or that give you something to think about.

You may find yourself being turned on by something you hadn't previously considered sexy or even sexual. And some of you may be turned on not so much by what is written about as by how it is written—these true tales of gay desire have a strong literary bent.

A lot of factors combine to float each of our boats, and there are no right or wrong responses—a reality that shaped the framework of this book: We wanted to know what turns *you* on; we wanted to know what turns *us* on collectively as gay men; we wanted the erotics of queer life to be used as a launching point for reflections on the queer condition; we wanted essays exploring the diverse manifestations of desire between and among men.

And whether they describe the intensity of a sexual experience that lingers forever or the ephemera of emotional desire that never leads to physical pleasure, that's what our thirty-four contributors offer—an unexpected zing of erotic excitement that mirrors what they've experienced.

Richard Labonté, Bowen Island, Canada
Lawrence Schimel, Madrid, Spain

Big Black Daddy-Dick, or, The Joys of Being Fetishized

Larry Duplechan

I learned the truth at seventeen. Well, actually, I had just turned eighteen. And I was just a few minutes and maybe three Levi's 501 buttons away from relinquishing my burdensome virginity to a cute, thirty-year-old crew-cut blond dude. He was the district manager of the McDonald's where I was working part-time. He was also coincidentally named Larry. It was my freshman year in college (UCLA to be specific), and I was standing against the kitchen counter in the studio apartment I was then sharing with a nelly but insistently heterosexual French and Linguistics double major, whose parents were pals with mine. Larry was squatting in front of me, struggling with those buttons on my Levi's. Finally, he managed to get my pants undone, and wrestled my bloated boybone from the confines of my Jockey shorts.

His pale blue eyes widened. His lips went slack, and then slowly curled up into a smile. At last, he said, "Wow!"

That's when I knew I had a big one.

Before that, I honestly hadn't known. I'd never compared in the locker room in high school: My abject terror that I might have an unwanted erection at school was sufficient to keep my dick all but concave, and my eyes focused downward. I don't believe I actually saw another boy's penis in four years of high school gym, though I did see a lot of bare feet, which may or may not have contributed to my foot fetish—but that's another essay. I'd always liked the look and feel of my own hard dick, but what boy doesn't? It was mine, after all; and it had afforded me a good deal of pleasure for years before I learned it could do the same for others. But Larry's "Wow!" answered a question that had nettled me for years: Was it big enough? That "Wow!" told me it was plenty big enough; and my sexual history has since been played out to a soundtrack of "Wow!", "Damn!", "Oh my God!", and "What the hell am I supposed to do with that thing?" (the last was voiced in the spring of 1976 by the young man who would become my boyfriend, my life partner, and finally my husband—fortunately, he figured out what to do with it rather quickly).

So, how big is it? I assumed you'd ask. And frankly, I don't know exactly. I have never applied a tape measure, ruler, or caliper to my dong. To paraphrase Eddie Murphy, white guys seem to be somewhat overly concerned with numbers; a Brother just looks down and says, "The shit is big." Neither have I any snapshots of my dick stretched out next to beer cans, portable telephones, or remote control devices, for comparison purposes.

But guys who have been there and taken measurements manual, oral, or otherwise seem to agree that it's about nine inches long, and about six inches around, which is what I tell guys online when they ask—and they almost invariably ask (as I've said, white guys really like their numbers). So, while my wang has been described as "huge" and "a monster," in fact it is neither. I have seen the occasional huge monster cock, and mine is not one of them. Still, it's a nice big wienie with a fat head and a wicked back-curve that a lot of guys really like (both to look at and to feel with various parts of their anatomies); and while it has always had its admirers (at least from the age of eighteen on), it is only since the advent of the Internet, and my own near-addiction to it, that my meat has gone global. Before the Internet, I had indulged my exhibitionism (and I am an exhibitionist, not a nudist—any actual nudist will tell you there's a big difference) at clothing-optional gay men's resorts in the Palm Springs desert; at nude cocktail parties, pool parties, massage parties, and movie nights organized by CMEN (California Men Enjoying Naturism) and LANG (Los Angeles Nude Guys); during occasional forays to bathhouses, and even less frequent forays into sex clubs (one memorable evening in a Mexico City sex club, native boys literally stood in line to take a look and grab a feel—apparently, they don't see a lot of black dick in Mexico City). But as nearly everyone knows, the 'net is Exhibitionism Central; it is my personal favorite playroom. After all, I can engage in hot sexplay with hundreds of men, hundreds of men at a time if I wanted to, and remain completely safe. As close to a perfect world as I can think of.

I think it is safe to assert that nothing has contributed as much to the shrinking of the world as the 'net. And on a personal level, were there no such thing as online video chat, I never would have dreamed that there were so many men in the world with a fetish for big black dick. Just ask a man who owns one. Sitting back in my towel-covered desk chair, lighting and camera angle adjusted for maximum effect, I am the Denzel of dick. I have been offered cash, airfare to the East Coast, and (I jive you not) marriage by men who seemed to care not a whit what I might look like from the neck up. Apparently, there are a certain number of white (though not exclusively white) gay (though, oddly enough, not always gay) men whose fascination with big black dick is sufficiently focused to render things like a face quite unimportant. Not surprisingly, I have found that big black dick is at a particular premium in places where there are relatively few actual black men: I'm very popular in Holland, Germany, the Scandinavian countries, the former Soviet Union, and Israel.

Middle age has, if anything, increased my fan base. A larger-than-usual dingdong, combined with a certain amount of lean muscle mass and my staunch refusal ever to lie about my age (fifty-two and counting), even online, has in recent years elevated me to the ranks of Big-Dicked Black Muscle Daddy. Who knew? A sissyboy in childhood, I tend to think of my midlife self as not-fem (hardly butch, but not fem), at best. But I have found that a nice set of pecs and a big sausage go a very long way toward butching up a middle-aged man in the eyes of others. Even in the ears of others, it seems;

men have inexplicably described my soft lyric-tenor speaking voice as "manly" and "sexy," particularly when intoning such monologues as "That's right, Boy—take that big black daddy-dick." Go figure.

And in this context, the category of "Boy" (and the desire to submit to "big black daddy-dick") can encompass a truly astounding range of age, size, and physical type. While I do seem to get an inordinate amount of play from young, slender white guys (eighteen to thirty-five), one of my online "Boys" on *dudesnude.com* is a forty-five-year-old, balding, beefy, hairy-chested, mustached musclebear (Italian-American but living in Hawaii). He loves to talk about "Daddy's monster cock," and begs me to fuck his "Boypussy" dry and "make little rips in my hole so I'm sure Daddy's seed enters my bloodstream faster—mark me as yours, inside and out."

A thick, furry, handsome thirty-something cub in Northern California has taken to calling himself my "Cockslave." He calls me "Master" or "SIR" in all-caps. (What is it with subs and "SIR" in all-caps?) While he claims to be mostly a top, he tells me that the moment he saw it, he realized it was his destiny to worship my big black cock. He continually expresses his desire to be my "bitchboy," and describes his need for my dick as one would an addiction: "I'm jonesin' for your cock, Master," and "I need your cock so bad, SIR," and, "Your cock is my weakness."

I was recently trading tales of online sexual goings-on with a buddy of mine (a gay white man), who asked me if I (an intelligent, college-educated, published novelist) didn't feel somewhat demeaned by being, as he put it, "objectified and fetishized." Did it not bother me, he wondered, being reduced to a mere penis, even a relatively impressive one? And I had to admit that, on the contrary, it turns me the fuck on. Big-time. I have a husband and at least my fair share of friends, all of whom know, love, and value me for the intelligent, articulate, many-splendored evolved person that I am. Sometimes, it's a lot of fun to be seen just as a big hot slab of fuckmeat. As a former sissy and ex-high-school band nerd, spindly and bespectacled, and getting by on personality and a knack for the well-aimed wisecrack, being admired, desired, indeed worshiped for the size and shape of my middle-aged johnson is a real kick. And yes, I have been worshiped. More on that a bit later.

Which is not to say that I don't have my limits. Some of these admirers/desirers/worshipers can get a little weird for my taste. A tall, pretty, twenty-ish white boy in Toronto recently wrote me: "I would love to see you rape someone, preferably a girl." Um ... no, thanks. Gay here. And I don't do rape—you gotta want it.

A tall, willowy, thirty-ish Southern queen stopped an online flirtation dead in its tracks by writing, "A hundred years ago, you'd have been lynched for touching me, and now I want your big nasty black cock in my pure white boypussy." Sorry, but the mention of lynching just doesn't get me going.

And when a young professional bodybuilder (blond and ripped and very likely on a 24/7 'roid high) expressed his desire for me to beat him with my fists while I pounded his truly transcendent ass, I couldn't go there (not even online, not even in my head). When I told him I really didn't get into beatings, he inquired, "How about if I called you Nigger?" When I replied, "Oh hell no," he came back with, "Please SIR. Please Nigger. Please Nigger SIR!" Just FYI, the "N-word" is a major soft-on for me.

Which doesn't mean that I'm in any sort of denial of the obvious racial element to this whole big black daddy-dick phenomenon. I mean, the word "black" is part of it, after all. And while a few of my daddy-worshiping Boys are of color, the vast majority of them are white. And if I claimed that the thought, let alone the sight, of a white man kneeling at my feet or on all fours submitting body and mind to my BBDD wasn't a huge turn-on, at least in part because the man below me was white, I would be less than honest. There, I've said it.

But about the worship thing:

By far the most imaginative, and consequently some of the most exciting online missives I have yet received have come from a twenty-something-year-old bareback bottom boy in Amsterdam.

A pretty, pouty-lipped white boy, "Gerritt" (not his real name, natch) is a self-proclaimed "black supremacist." While others call me Daddy and Master and SIR, Gerritt went so far as to declare me his god. No, really.

He posted on his *dudesnude.com* profile the announcement that "I have a new god, and it is (my *dudesnude.com* screen name—and if you want it, you'll just have to ask me for it). No one will be granted access to my boypussy without his permission." Since we lived half the planet apart, Gerritt chose to submit to my "Blessed Ebony Phallus" (his term) by granting me the final word on who from *dudesnude* he would and would not submit to in the flesh. For months, I did little else than answer emails from horny Dutchmen and hopeful visitors to The Netherlands, seeking permission to fuck my Boy. And make no mistake, sometimes I said no. And my word was final. Gerritt would email me and report the occasional fool who actually thought he might work around me. (I mean, come on—a real top respects that the Master-Boy relationship is sacred, even from thousands of miles away.) It got to be so much work (Gerritt is a beautiful boy and he got a lot of offers) that I finally commanded (a man asks, a god commands) that Gerritt decide for himself who was and wasn't worthy to taste the fruits of my "Sacred Temple Whore, the ever-pregnant Receptacle of the Holy Black Seed" (he came up with that little turn of phrase, as well—this kid's got an imagination on him).

When I commanded he take and send me photos of himself bent over, spreading his porcelain-white ass cheeks and displaying his rosebud, he obeyed quickly (as a good Boy should). His cover email (Subject line: "Offering to a Black God") was a verse from his very own nasty-boy Bible:

"Everlasting Saviour, Horny Spirit, and Breeder Almighty, I want to say thanks for granting me a glimpse into Your Horny Cumdom. As my God requested, I sent some pix of my cunt lips, my pussy dedicated to my Lord. Had to pay the amateur photographer with sex ... sex is always good and yesterday especially, because it was a way to service my God. In my mind I heard the Lord's Voice: give yourself to glorify and fulfill the will of your God."

Now, I'm a good Christian boy, raised in the black Baptist church. I'm a deacon at Metropolitan Community Church in the Valley. I can imagine very few things so perverted, so sacrilegious, so basically and patently wrong, and consequently so cock-throbbing, pre-cum leaking hot as the boldfaced blatant blasphemy of this little Dutch slutboy elevating my cock to the position of an idol god. I mean, didn't people used to get turned into salt for this sort of thing? Gerritt's libidinous imagination is epitomized in the following phallic psalm:

Hail to Thee,
Magnificent and Mighty Black Cock!
To Thee do I bow and pray.

All Glory and Adoration
to your Magnificent Form.
To Thee do I bow and pray.

Worship and praise to Thee,
Splendor of all Mankind.
To Thee do I bow and pray.

Oh bless me Lord God Black Cock.
Fill me with Your seed, for
To Thee do I bow and pray.

Hail Black Cock.
Hail Black Cock.
Hail Black Cock. Amen.

Wow! Now, if you'll excuse me, I need to … um … wash my hands.

Tom Selleck's Mustache

Jay Neal

I was not born a cocksucker. I acquired skill at that delectable pas-
time through diligent study and long hours of pleasurable practice. Neither was I born a ready-made bottom, thereby skewing the
alleged demographics of most major cities but avoiding the unre-
lieved burden of searching for the perfect top.

No, my desire for man-to-man love, and man-to-man sex, revealed itself to me painfully slowly by means of romantic visions,
absurdly like the cover illustrations of dime-store romance novels,
in which I was swept into the strong and caring arms of hunky
men whom I then kissed madly, deeply, and passionately for hours
and hours. (I was a little vague on exactly what came next.) That
was how I knew The Kiss (capital letters, please) has ever been the
touchstone of my romantic and sexual being.

Oddly, my glance does not immediately fall on a man's lips. The
lips, the tongue, and the mouth, for all their sensuous splendor,
have little visual erotic appeal for me. Instead, all of my attention
focuses entirely on that tiny expanse of landscape just above his
lips. When I look on the face of desire, I see his mustache.

I have always been attracted to men with facial hair, but realizing
that attraction took some time. Recognizing that it was way out of
the ordinary took substantially longer.

My awakening began in 1972, my seventeenth year, during the
hormone-drenched summer following my sophomore year in high
school. That was the summer of the Games of the XX Olympiad,
the Olympics in Munich, West Germany, the summer of Mark
Spitz's mustache.

Mark Spitz was twenty-two that year, a brash but talented young swimmer who went to the games predicting that he would win six gold medals. He didn't—he won seven. His achievement made him an American hero. He gained instant celebrity and his face was seen everywhere, instantly recognizable for the mustache that he wore—a mustache frequently described as "iconic"—at a time when any sort of facial hair was thought an exotic or suspicious affectation. For me, the constant barrage of images of Spitz and Spitz's mustache provided a non-stop frisson. At that age a hard-on would present itself with the least provocation and here was enough provocation to create a continual conundrum: there were hardly enough hours in the day to jerk off. And that was before the appearance of *the poster*.

An instant best-seller, the poster featured swim-buff Spitz dressed only in his winning "Star-Spangled" Speedo, accessorized with 1) his seven Olympic gold medals arrayed across his bare chest, and 2) his mustache. One's eyes were presumably meant to linger on the medals; mine did not. As a fledgling faggot with an emerging fetish for Lycra, my gaze might well have lingered on his swimwear and what it barely concealed. In truth, though, I was transfixed by his mustache. Vague romantic fantasies of kissing ensued.

I never bought my own copy of the Mark Spitz poster. I could blame a lack of ready cash for something so frivolous, but I imagine I really avoided buying it in order to avoid any hint that I might be obsessing about this thrilling image of a near-naked, mustachioed man. Instead, I had to find excuses to go to the shopping mall and manufacture pretexts that allowed me to keep walking past the poster display at Spencer Gifts, stealing glances and storing them up in my mind until I was back home in my darkened bedroom, where I could replay the vision at my self-pleasuring leisure. This was surely the stuff dreams were made on. I wonder how many orgasms across America came at the hands of that poster.

I was a late developer and never slated for great accomplishment in the hirsute category. The appearance of each additional pubic hair was cause for celebration—and I celebrated with friends when-ever I could. Growing any body hair at all seemed an unattainable goal.

During my junior year in high school one of my classmates—only one!—had a real mustache, a luxurious, trimmable growth of upper-lip hair that shamed the wispy wannabe mustaches that barely made an impression on the faces of the rest of us. Clearly this guy shaved. Regularly! He also had visible chest hair, and was a football hero who dated the most popular cheerleader in the school. It was clear proof that all good things came to those with body hair.

Provided, of course, that one did not have too much body hair. A light spray of hair scattered casually across one's chest was a much desired treasure. Perversely, a very hairy body was thought by most of my contemporaries to be a curse. Hairy toes or fingers, a hairy back, or worst of all, hairy shoulders were deemed ultra-high in ickiness and cause for permanent social ostracism.

Though I didn't come within miles of the hairy-shoulder af-fliction, I was not a great social success since, by that time, I was a fully developed dork and generally acclaimed a Tinkerbell, an epithet whose full euphemistic impact escaped me then. As a so-cial outsider, I was a ready-made confidant for Dave, the hairiest of the hairy-shouldered pariahs at our school. As luck would have it—luck, or the taunting forces of a cruelly ironic universe—our schedules crossed in the locker room between our summer swim classes. We became locker room buddies.

To developing but timid young homos like me, the locker room could be undeniably exciting and unbearably terrifying at the same time. It was about the only legitimate occasion where one could see naked guys without contrivance. That was highly desirable. At the same time there were all those naked guys, so the threat of popping a boner was ever present. This bit of locker room logic was clearly understood by all: if naked guys, then boner, therefore homo. A hard-on in the locker room was a throbbing, pulsing, neon arrow pointing the way to everlasting shame.

And so circumstances threw Dave and me together socially. I stayed late in the locker room, dawdling as much as I credibly could to avoid changing in front of all the other guys as an erection-avoidance tactic. Dave was still in the locker room when the others had left partly because it took longer for him to dry his vast abundance of hairy skin.

I say "partly" because, as I sat on the bench listening to Dave and he propped a leg on the bench to dry his thigh, crotch, and butt crack, it dawned on me that his toweling activity seemed to pass beyond mere drying into the realm of unabashed pleasure. I cannot claim with certainty that he was alternately displaying his deliciously hairy butt-cheeks, his meaty dick, or well-furred balls simply for my enjoyment, but it was a good operating theory that fit the facts. He never complained about my looking, and I certainly had no complaints.

Call it imprinting, call it catalysis, even call it recruiting if you like, but my semi-erotic encounters with Dave confirmed the diagnosis triggered by Mark Spitz's mustache: I longed to be kissed by men; I wanted my men hairy; and there would be mustaches.

In addition to being the year of Spitz, 1972 was the year that the relatively obscure Burt Reynolds posed for photographs in *Cosmopolitan* wearing nothing but his mustache. Then, in 1976, the mustache of the pleasantly furry Sam Elliott starred in the movie *Lifeguard*. With Elliott playing the title role mostly unclothed most of the time, who cared how weak the plot was?

For better or worse, disco surged in the 1970s, with none surging more than the music of the Village People and the mustaches of Victor Willis (cop), Glenn Hughes (biker), Randy Jones (cowboy), David Hodo (construction worker), and Alex Briley (sailor). The costumes were cute but the mustaches were hot, particularly Hughes' extravagant handlebar. Later, my allegiance to musical mustaches would belong to Freddie Mercury—who wouldn't love the lips of a mouth that could sing like that?

About the same time, the Castro-clone look with its *de rigueur* mustache was sprouting in San Francisco. However, we in the Midwest were culturally as far from that leading edge of gay fashion as we were far from Oz, still very much in Kansas.

Then the fall of 1980 arrived and with it the mustache of Tom Selleck, star of the television series *Magnum, P.I.* The series was top-rated throughout its amazing eight-year run, a popularity that I suspect can only be attributed to Selleck's mustache and the broad expanse of his hairy chest, displayed with the least excuse. People were forever wanting to talk to him urgently when he was swimming, changing clothes, or just stepping out of the shower, all of which he did with unusual frequency for a television character.

I don't remember whether I jerked off during episodes, but I can't imagine why I wouldn't have done so. My mental catalog of sexual techniques was still not very advanced at the time, so there was no "Oh Magnum, feed me your load!" or "Deeper, Magnum, harder!" fantasies going on. Not at all. At that time, my epitome of sexual desire, my most urgent longing, was for The Kiss.

Kissing is still—even after all these years, all the positions, all the techniques, all the experiments—the pinnacle of my sexual satisfaction, and nothing is more satisfying than kissing a man with facial hair: the mustache pricks one's lips with countless bristly hairs. It's better therapy than a thousand acupuncture needles. Beard burn of the lips creates the warmest, most persistent afterglow. Nothing curls my toes like long, deep kissing.

Timidity and career demands gave me plenty of excuses to repress my desires, so my journey to sexual maturity and real, grown-up relationships was slow and long, though not particularly tortured or tortuous. It was several years after my one-sided—and one-handed—affair with Tom Selleck's mustache before I finally consummated my yearnings with the man I think of tenderly as my first one-night stand.

In today's vernacular he was an otter: lean and lithe and covered with dark, fine-textured body hair. Lovely to look at, luscious to hold. He had a dick, of course, a magnificent one that functioned quite well as I recall, but you will not be surprised that my attention, all of my pent-up desire, was entirely directed towards his mouth.

He had a beautiful, black, and delightfully bristly Van Dyke beard. His short black hair, smoldering dark-brown eyes, and narrow, V-shaped face gave him a vaguely sinister appearance in a Vincent Price-ish way. He looked a little debauched, like the faun in *Allegro non troppo*. These were characteristics I deemed greatly to his advantage.

Predictably, my most vital memory of our brief but highly charged encounter is of our snuggling together on my couch, still with all of our clothes on. He lay lupine on my chest, staring into my eyes with incendiary intent. We touched lips, we brushed beards, we opened mouths to taste tongues. We kissed and kissed until we were breathless—and then we kissed some more until our lips were so sore we could tolerate no more. Years of fantasy and longing poured into my kissing, and I was unstoppable. Fortunately, my partner was a willing and capable companion for my much anticipated exploration. Who knew that the interior of the mouth could have so much territory to discover?

Obviously, the question is rhetorical: From long experience with innumerable dry runs in my own mind, I knew The Kiss was an infinite frontier I could travel with endless satisfaction and never tire. I knew, too, that mustaches and beards were the landmarks that would border my route.

Thus my track was set along the trail of the hirsute. Not long after my first one-night stand, I came upon what I hadn't even known I'd been looking for. I discovered bears and felt for the first time like Baby Bear must have felt in Goldilocks' cabin: I'd found a spot to settle in that was just right.

Choice Cuts: My Other Erotic Bio

Zachary Taylor

> Every person has two erotic biographies. Usually people talk only about the first, the list of affairs and one-night stands. The other biography is sometimes more interesting ...
> —*Milan Kundera*

Manhattan, Port Authority Bus Terminal, eight p.m. on a sultry evening in late August 1990. The first Gulf War has just begun, my reserve unit has been mobilized, and I'm headed, eventually, for Kuwait. I'm sitting by myself in the rear of the bus, feeling conspicuous in my army officer's uniform—a magnet for moms and pops moved by empathy, veterans with tales of long-ago wars, and zombied-out teens with headphones. I avert my eyes from the still-boarding passengers, aware of the army corporal only as he stands at the edge of my seat, asking, "Sir, is this seat free?" With a sense of relief, I say, "Yes, corporal." He rambles, explaining, "I could sit somewhere else, sir, but all the other seats are, well ..." I cut him short. I pat the seat emphatically, insistent. "Sit here, corporal, I know what you're saying."

He stretches over and above me to make space for his duffle in an already overstuffed rack, repeating, "Sorry, sir," while he rummages. I'm aware of his trim midsection, the starchy scent of his cotton khakis. I notice innocent muscles bulging like hidden weapons under his shirt, the contour of his cock where it touches his pants. He is totally squared away, from buzz cut to spit-shined shoes. Dropping gracefully into his seat, he sighs, "Thank you, sir," prompting me to insist, "It's Zachary, corporal, call me Zack." With a broad smile on his ruddy, lantern-jawed face, he wraps a strong hand around mine, pumping it while gently mimicking me: "Giovanni, sir—call me John." We proceed to organize legs, arms, and torsos, as if to mark space where space is indivisible.

With a leg and arm awkwardly bent to avoid contact with mine, he announces solemnly, "I've figured it out, sir. With me and you both over six feet, we've got to pack twenty-four feet of bones into nine cubic feet—that's including four arms and four legs, of course." I like his anatomical riddle, the dry humor.

"You're saying it's undoable then?"

"I would say so, yessir."

I give his knee a quick, hard jab with mine, "Then we've got to loosen up. Can you loosen up, John?"

He jabs back with *his* knee, only harder, suggesting, "What do you say we don't count arms and legs, sir?"

"A deal," I tell him. "And try to remember to call me Zack."

The doors of the bus close with a whoosh, the overhead lights go out, the a/c blasts on high, and we begin our roughly three-hour journey to Dover, Delaware, and the air force base that will be our ultimate point of departure. Pulling out of the concourse and making a circular ascent on the great concrete cloverleaf, the bus pushes onto the congested highway and into a sudden downpour, with flashes of lightning illuminating the heads of passengers like apparitions and thunder rumbling over the Palisades. Outside, eighteen-wheelers float in the spray, which strikes the sides of the bus with the force of a bullwhip. Beyond the highway lies a garish landscape of flashing lights and tall smokestacks rimmed with flame. The scene is unreal, hellish, emboldening us somehow, like an invitation to a party in Hades. We settle in, letting our limbs conform to the motion of the bus and the logic of desire. Our knees and thighs are touching, our hard-ons the barometer of our desire.

We share an easy camaraderie, talking matter-of-factly about things that bond us. We're both New Yorkers, graduates of rival high schools. I played soccer, he was a wrestler. At nineteen (him) and twenty-three (me), we're not that far apart in age. I went to college, he didn't, assured of a future in the storied butcher shop that his family has run in Little Italy for three generations. "Choice and specialty cuts," he says proudly. Smiling, I resist a smutty play on words, but he reads me anyway, smiling back. We talk about the "scene," our old buddies and hangouts, gay bars and clubs. We talk about the war, its trauma and trivia, for now we fancy ourselves warriors. He joined the army "to think things over, get a handle, learn self-discipline."

As we talk, he raises his left leg, positioning his foot just below the armrest of the seat before him. His forearm settles on his knee, obscuring a major line of sight. He scans the coach and its occupants systematically, as a sniper might do, head and eyes moving deliberately, front to rear, side to side, missing no detail. And without skipping a beat in his role as spotter, he smoothly slides his right hand onto and around my thigh, squeezing tightly, then tracing the contour of my stiff cock with his fingers. "Fuck!" he says in frustration. "I want to get physical with you so bad. Want to wrestle you nude, control you with my fast moves, whatever it takes. And I want to see if you can take me down."

Regardless of where our gaze is directed, searching out potential threat, our *sotto voce* conversation is unbroken. On the exterior we are calmness itself. Inside we simmer, as desire morphs into lust. With care, he unzips my fly, sliding his hand inside, through the opening of my boxers, encircling my cock with his fingers, lubing the head with his thumb and my pre-cum, removing his hand, sucking his thumb, and repeating the ritual. Our eyes meet, I cover his hand with mine, pressing down on my crotch, telling him, "I want to get physical, too, with fast moves of my own. Fair warning." Removing my cock from my pants, he grasps it firmly, slowly, slowly jacking. I feel a rush, push my head deep into the headrest, looking straight ahead, pulse racing, sweating. The air is sick with desire.

There is no sense of time as we edge each other physically, verbally, endlessly. We take a break, get out of our seats and casually walk the aisle like two surveyors, assuring ourselves that the two GIs stretched out in the back row are sleeping. Now I take the outside seat, becoming both sentry and predator. With my eyes scanning the aisle, my hand advances to his crotch, where I wrap it around his already exposed thick meat, standing at attention in readiness. "Specialty or choice?" I ask him. Ignoring my levity, he says, "It's beyond belief, this feeling. Just with you—no one else. Why is that?"

I'm lost in my obsession with his tool, handling it almost clinically, feeling the heft, the pulsing veins, softly slapping the shaft with the palm of my hand, staking my claim on his flesh. Slowly, carefully, I circle the moist glans with my thumb, pausing, resuming, pausing, but unintentionally bringing him to a critical point and an urgent reaction: "Easy! Wait! Wait!" We change the subject, we exchange addresses, anything to dampen the fire, the hammering in the head, the gnawing ache in the crotch, the blue balls, and the craving without relief.

The ending comes abruptly, with lights up a half hour before arrival, and the driver announcing the first stop—our stop. Passengers awake from slumber. Some, including the two of us, stand, reaching for baggage, readying ourselves. Even though we are both getting off here, we hug—a strong bear hug, faces touching, stubble rubbing stubble, unembarrassed. Within minutes, we find ourselves inside a stark, harshly lit receiving area, where officers and enlisted men go their designated way.

Six months later, when he was in Iraq and I was in Kuwait, I received a hot letter from him, in which he referred to one of two letters I'd written him. He wrote, "Your letter and your picture keep rolling though my mind." He had enclosed a full-length photo of himself in uniform, looking leaner, less innocent, with a discreet bulge in his crotch. On the back he had written, "You will know why." I wrote two more letters, and I imagine he wrote, too, but fast-moving events proved a challenge even for the Army Post Office.

A year later, after I was discharged, and within hours of settling in with a buddy in SoHo, I headed for Little Italy and the butcher shop. The address was now a pizzeria whose owner had bought out the lease through an agent. A waiter in a nearby restaurant, an old-timer, told me the old man had sold out and moved to Baltimore, where he had family. He knew nothing about the son's where-abouts. That was it. I could have contacted the Army Department, of course, but I let it ride, swept along by work and relationships, totally convinced we would meet one day on the street, in a bar or club, or at the San Gennaro Festival.

Now, nearly twenty years later, John, a.k.a "Choice Cuts," looms large in my "second erotic biography," as Czech novelist Milan Kundera calls that "mournful history" of those we wanted but who eluded us. And when I replay the episode in memory or fantasy, I wonder if there could be an experience more indelible than the frustration of animal lust—a condition so rarefied and all-consum-ing that the lustful merit their own circle in Hades. Fulfillment can be bliss, yes, but frustration burns as hot as a branding iron, leaving its imprint on the brain, somewhere in the region of our survival instincts, no doubt.

As Kundera says, our "other" erotic biography can be more in-teresting than the "real" one. For one thing, the others, the absent ones, can be stronger aphrodisiacs than lovers present in the flesh, with all their baggage and pressing needs. And even without our knowledge, those absent ones occupy territory, stake a claim on our sexuality, shaping our relationships in real life. Sometimes, in fact, they are combatants waging guerrilla warfare behind our backs.

When Eros Meets Daddy

Daniel Gawthrop

I envy the polymorphously perverse: the people who can, who will, have sex with just about anyone. The notion of being erotically uninhibited while exercising discernment in one's choices strikes me as a condition of supreme enlightenment. I'm similarly envious of bisexuals: their ability to respond to beauty, regardless of gender, makes them more trustworthy on matters of discrimination—not less—than heteros or homos. When I look at my own erotic track record, I cannot begin to claim this degree of enlightenment. For one thing, I'm limited to men. For another, I have discriminatory tastes in at least one important aspect. Not race (I don't want to die until I've tasted a hot guy from every corner of the planet) and not class (I'm as quick to bed a yuppie as a yard worker). No, the second barrier that prevents me from claiming status as a fully realized sexual being is age.

From my first pubescent erection onward, I have never consummated an erotic encounter with someone much older than myself. Even as a young man coming out of the closet—a period where sex with one's elders should be inevitable, given the tutoring required to navigate such a passage—I always made sure never to end an evening alone with an older man. At the same time, I accepted drinks, dinner invitations, concert tickets, out-of-town trips, job references, useful contacts, and other forms of hospitality from all sorts of older men who wanted me. I realize this makes me no different from anyone else whose youthful salad days were marked by freeloading opportunism. But even then I was rather extreme in my tastes: at twenty-five, I was a chicken hawk among chicken, a youthful ephebophile whose age range for desirable lovers was barely legal to twenty-five. As I grew older the range expanded—but never beyond my own years.

Why was it so hard to share my body with someone older? Was it really so precious a gift to give away? Why could I not appreciate the experience these men had to offer, both between the sheets and out in the world? Did I not see the advantage that a fling with an elder might give me, in so many different ways? Or was I too much of a control queen to risk vulnerability with someone who had the wisdom to see right through me?

I know what you're thinking: *Now that he's reached middle age, he's finally realizing that he doesn't turn heads like he once did. In fact, he's let his body go quite a bit. But despite the flab, and the rather sad wardrobe he uses to conceal it, he still expects young cuties to pay attention to him and pathetically resents the fact they ignore him. So now, at last, he can identify with those old guys he used to take advantage of. Now he can afford to wag his finger self-righteously and tut-tut the sin of ageism. Well, cry me an effing river* ... Fair enough. Guilty as charged.

I wish I could have been attracted to older men. It might have made things easier during my freelance days, when I lived month to month on hundred-dollar book reviews and auto show features for insurance magazines. It was during this period, in my late twenties and early thirties, that I wondered what it might be like to sleep one's way to success—in the manner of some Hollywood model-cum-starlet or the office girl who becomes head of the corporation. (Did anyone actually do that?) Once you got past the mercenary crudeness, the vulgarity of the exchange—career advancement for a bit of naked frolicking—it all seemed rather daring and glamorous. But then I'd remember what end of the exchange I was on, and the idea was no longer so appetizing. Because, after all, newspaper editors, TV producers, and book publishers aren't all that different from Hollywood directors or corporate CEOs; they don't tend to look like Josh Hartnett. Still, all these years later, I can't help won-

dering what might have happened if I had allowed myself to be se-
duced by some of the greybeards, Daddy figures, and older-brother
types who courted me in my youth.

It would at least have made for good gossip if I'd been more
charming with a future award-winning British novelist who I met
one day while looking for freelance work in London during the
early 1990s. This salt-and-pepper-haired scribe in his late forties
had a well-known yen for young men. At least his protagonists did,
which is why I was mildly alarmed when, within minutes of our
introduction, he was inviting me to a garden party the following
weekend. "Oh, that would be nice," I said. But I was spooked. I had
visited his office at a highbrow literary journal in an ambitious quest
to find writing leads. And here he was, putting the moves on me;
undressing me with his eyes, barely registering a word I was saying, asking if I liked garden parties, and then inviting me to be his
date. Imagining what kind of a lover he might be, I felt smothered
by his Oxbridge airs—almost as oppressive as the cologne wafting
from his tweed vest. He must have sensed my panic, for he quickly
changed tack and reverted to the stiffly formal. Repeating his journal's editorial policy in a manner that made it clear there were no
freelance openings for a barefoot colonial, he put a damper on my
ambition by offering no hint of where else I might look. By the end
of our meeting he was brushing me off with exquisitely English
decorum as he led me to the door. "Perhaps we'll meet again one
day." So much for writing leads. Perhaps I should have put my hand
on his thigh.

Another British writer in his forties, an art critic for one of London's quality broadsheets, was more transparent in his attraction.
A., to whom I was introduced by a mutual friend in Vancouver,
treated me to dinner and took me for long walks along the Thames,
regaling me with Edwardian monologues about the meaning of
beauty. He also had a naughty sense of humor. One night, in a gesture of arch irony, he took me to a Chippendales show and decided
to review it. We were the only two men in a theater packed with

screaming housewives. After the show, we laughed about those horny women all the way to the Tube station where we parted. Given how well we were getting along, and how generous A. had been in squiring me about town, I felt badly that I could not take these evenings where he ultimately wanted them to go—which was back to his apartment. What could I say? A. wasn't that bad looking, was well-dressed, and had impeccable taste in just about everything. But what was I going to do with all that body hair? Or those wrinkles? Or that world-weary sadness, which, beneath all the wit, gave his ardor a hint of desperation? At that time, my lovers included a twenty-year-old black rugby player I'd picked up in Hampstead Heath and a Thai fashion designer from Highgate who allowed me to fuck him on his studio floor. With all that youthful transgression on offer, who needed middle-aged vanilla?

With a few older men, I did allow physical contact, but the result was never satisfying for either party, not least because of the alcohol involved. There was the professor from a local university I'd gotten to know, along with his partner, over the course of several dinner parties they hosted. I understood that the professor, who was in his late sixties, took a shine to me, and I accepted his warmth and flattery as any good son would. But on one occasion, when I was too drunk to leave and agreed to stay the night, the professor followed me down the hallway and copped a feel before I closed the bedroom door. Part of me wanted to please him, but another part would have felt sordid doing anything under his partner's nose, so I swatted him away. In another case, a radio personality who invited me to dinner waited until his other guests had left before taking me upstairs to the roof of his downtown apartment. To this day, I cannot recall how he managed to get me on my knees, giving him a blowjob, since the idea seemed as ludicrous then as it does now. All I remember is that I had to stop after a minute and—apologizing for my lack of enthusiasm, as if turning down one of his dessert plates—attempt a graceful exit. I never did get another dinner invite.

Am I saying that if I'd given in to those British literary men and the sex had been stellar, I'd be signing six-figure deals and thanking all those Booker judges by now? Hardly. But there is something to be said for being open to the kind of sexual experience that does not lead to instant gratification. Selfless sex is like any other charitable act of good will: it might take a lot of effort on your part, and it might even seem an inconvenience, but the fact that your effort is appreciated by the recipient is what makes the effort worthwhile. The appreciation, when genuinely expressed, should be satisfaction enough. Yes, this is news to the narcissist who builds an entire erotic life based on selfish ("How do I feel about this?") sex. I gained some insight into this idea every time I visited a bathhouse and found myself the youngest man on the premises. On most nights, I would hold my ground and touch no one until someone who fell within a decade of acceptability showed up. But other times, I would find myself sitting in a steam room or standing in a dark room with only an older man beside me, and I would let go; just let him do whatever he pleased. Something told me I'd get extra karma points every time an older man left the room happy. One less rejection in that kind of place is good karma for everyone.

Having examined my conscience on this issue—and put my ass, quite literally, on the line to explore it—by age forty-five I had un-covered no deep, disturbing truth about my aversion to sex with elders. No problematic relationship with my father (we got along better than ever, and he was still raging at eighty-two); no legacy of abuse by Catholic priests or other authority figures in my youth (a minor miracle, really, given some of the pedophiles in circulation at the time); and no unhealthy fear of intimacy or loss of control (a select few lovers my own age and younger, I had found, could reach my inner core with little effort). If there was any secret to this pe-culiar phobia, it lay in a single encounter from 1988, when I was not quite twenty-five, with a forty-eight-year-old employer.

As far as tutors go, J. was formidable. Our politics couldn't have been more opposed—I was a budding social democrat, he a right-wing übercapitalist—but he knew how to push my buttons, and he passed along some important street knowledge when I needed it most. J. was a senior systems analyst who was subcontracted to an Alberta management consulting firm when he hired me as a technical writer. I had met him while changing trains in Winnipeg, halfway through a cross-country trek from Halifax a few days after finishing journalism school. He gave me his card; I called him up a couple of months later, when I couldn't find any newspaper jobs. He hired me on the spot.

J. was one of those William F. Buckley-meets-Gordon Gecko, *Masters-of-the-Universe* clichés of the 1980s: greed is good, the individual is king, etc. He drove a new Jaguar, rented a twenty-third floor condo in Calgary he said once belonged to Alberta premier Don Getty, charged $250 an hour for his knowledge of "third-generation database concepts," and boasted of being able to argue any side of a debate and win, thanks to his Jesuitical upbringing. It was this latter skill he used to great effect in getting into my pants. The seduction, which began from facing leather chairs in the dining room of J.'s condo, took the form of cross-examination masquerading as psychotherapy. J., also trained in Gestalt, wanted to get to the bottom of my odd, seemingly asexual behavior and decided that an aggressive round of interviewing would break the logjam. Once he confirmed I was queer, he set about trying to identify what turned me on.

"What kind of guy gives you a hard-on?" he asked clinically.

"River Phoenix," I said, without hesitation. I had just seen *A Night in the Life of Jimmy Reardon*, an otherwise forgettable, low-budget teen comedy that featured Phoenix in his first leading role, as a horny and duplicitous bad boy whose sexual escapades move most of the plot. The eighteen-year-old River's coming-of-age film was startling to behold, and so soon after the prepubescent earnestness of *Stand By Me*. Apart from talent, Phoenix possessed a James Dean-like pompadour, a pixie-like nose, and honeydew skin, which, combined with his raw, dissolute sexuality, made for serious eye candy. Very, very hot.

"All right then," said J. "I want you to close your eyes, think of River Phoenix, and put your hand in your pants."

"Huh! Why?"

"Because you're too uptight. You need to get in touch with your sexuality. Own it. Enjoy it. Don't be afraid of it."

"And why do I have to do that in front of you?"

"Because you clearly haven't done it in front of anyone else. It's about time you did."

From there, it was a short distance to the living room couch where, after putting on some dreadful Muzak by Mannheim Steamroller, J. knelt down in front of me as I lay on the black leather furniture, pulled down my boxer shorts, grabbed my cock, and began licking it.

"Just keep thinking of River Phoenix," he said, noting my lack of response.

"Maybe you should try the Fleetwood Mac," I replied, recalling the bouncing melody and Christine McVie's ethereal vocals in "Everywhere," which J. had blasted on the Jaguar's stereo while doing 140 km/h down the highway from Edmonton.

I did try to focus on River Phoenix, but I kept coming back to images of Don Getty and the Alberta Conservative Party, Old Boys' clubs with their vulgar jokes, cigars and whiskey, and J. himself: hypoglycemic, overweight, balding, and looking much older than forty-eight, with nothing in his fridge but a bag of Oreo cookies and a carton of milk six weeks past its expiry date. J., kneeling in front of me, his dome bobbing up and down on my cock. Finally, he gave up.

"All right then," he said, looking coldly into my eyes, "if you don't want to do it with me, that's fine. But you've got to do it with someone."

"How do you know I haven't done it with 'someone'?"

"Because you are so much like a cocker spaniel," he sneered.

"What do you mean?"

"I mean," he said, pulling my boxers back up and snapping the waist band onto my belly for added emphasis, "that you're all cute and earnest and innocent, but you're also kind of stupid. You know, oblivious. You have no idea what people want from you, but you'll go along with them anyway, allowing them to lead you into situations like this. Well, if you're going to work for me then you'd better figure out what turns you on and go and get it—and soon—because if you keep up this cocker spaniel routine you're going to get eaten alive by someone far worse than me. Think about it."

Yikes. It was true. I had been J.'s plaything before this evening. Why had he invited me into his compartment for a gin and tonic the moment we met at the train station in Winnipeg? Could it have been the way I took my shirt off while hauling my bags between trains, walking past him half-naked? Why had I not found anything strange about the fact he offered me work without knowing a thing about me? Or the fact that, when I finally called a few months later, he not only remembered me but took the call during a meeting and hired me on the spot? Was it normal for a technical writer to move into his boss's highrise apartment within two days of getting the job? Or for the boss to order him not to wear underwear during a meeting with other contractors because "flaunting your basket before the competition throws them off their game"?

J. had played me like a fiddle. But at least he was willing to tell me so and offer me another way of seeing the world. He knew that by confronting my closeted sexuality he was ultimately setting me free. And for that lesson, I could never thank this older man enough.

Three French Men

Shaun Levin

The cubicle

Number One would not kiss. His height and his body and his cock and his skin and his face and everything was just right—but in the steam room where we met, Number One turned his head when I went for his lips. He was an inch taller than me. His cock was hard and upright. His hair was black and his skin was pale. He was so skinny that when I put my arms around him I could touch my own shoulders; it was as if there was nothing there. Number One whispered (in French), "Let's go into a cubicle where we can be alone." I assume that's what he said when we left the steam room and he turned to see if I was following. Number One held my hand as we went upstairs. But Number One and I did not last very long. He seemed disappointed when I went to leave the cubicle he'd led us to. I didn't explain why I was leaving. (I rarely do.) I didn't say much except, "*Je veux ouvré la porte.*" If I'd been in London, which is now my home, but far from everywhere I've come from, I'd have said; "I rely on your lips against mine to stay erect." I'd have said something to make it clear that kissing was part of fucking. Number One is the one who would not kiss. He was tall and skinny—my favorite—and would have been the one I'd have fallen for. But I cannot bear the desertion of a kiss refused. And he didn't smile.

The steam room

Number Two liked to kiss very much. Number Two kissed with a hungry enthusiasm. He stood on tiptoes to kiss me. Number Two was short enough to suck my nipples from a standing position. He had the fattest cock. He was also the darkest—he could have been Portuguese; so many of the Portuguese men I've met have exceptionally large cocks, not unlike the thick fat cocks of some black men I've known from whom I'm sure those Portuguese are descended. Number Two liked sex a lot, he was into it, as opposed to needing someone to help him get off. He tried to lick my arse, but I hadn't showered, and I'd been shitting all morning (foreign cities make me nervous), though the real reason I avoided his tongue is that it takes me a while before I offer my arse to strangers. Number Two spoke to me in English; perhaps it was the couple of times I said, yeah, yeah, or maybe he couldn't speak French either. Maybe he was Portuguese. Number Two shaved his chest.

He kissed with gusto, the way he did everything, the way he made me pick him up so he could wrap his legs around my waist and rest his elbows on my shoulders. Number Two was a koala bear. He didn't care that there was no visible sign of my arousal. By visible sign I mean an erection. But he was nice to kiss and his cock made me think of those pictures some men have of their penises alongside an aerosol can or a can of Coke. Number Two's cock was like a can of Coke.

We were in the steam room, having both warded off the advances of a scruffy old man who'd been going around touching everyone, as if in some lethargic game of tag. I, too, was desperate for physical contact, and the wonder of his cock was a comfort and a pleasure in itself. It had the reassurance of an anchor. Number Two kept saying fuck me, fuck me, until the heat in the steam room became so unbearable we had to douse ourselves in cold water under the shower by the door.

When Number Two came—I'm assuming that's what the sound was—we kissed, and he said, "Take care" (in English). Of all three men I would encounter that day, Number Two was the most eager. Number Two might have smiled, but it was dark and misty, and I wasn't wearing my glasses, but going by his wholehearted behavior,

I wouldn't be surprised if Number Two was smiling.

The dry sauna

I was about to leave to go back to my hotel, so Number Three was unexpected. He was so perfect in his body, his cock, and his thuggish good looks that I didn't insist on the whole mouth-to-mouth thing. Kissing could wait. I was happy to adore, to be the supplicant. Number Three wanted someone to help him get off; his was the kind of beauty that made people want to service him. He said very few words; "non" and "Stefan" were two of them. He showed very little interest. A friend of mine says that indifference is a particularly French trait; they reserve their enthusiasm for food and ideas. But I need enthusiasm when I'm having sex. I need that wide-eyed effusive energy from my lovers. I need to see that my being there and their being there at that moment in time is a great joy. Enthusiasm is a form of cosmic gratitude. But I make exceptions.

Sometimes my enthusiasm is enough for two.

With Number Three, my enthusiasm was enough for two.

His appearance was a surprise. I'd been sitting on the wooden slats in the sauna and I'd been thinking. Number One and Number Two were fine. But third time lucky. And it was. Number Three was my third-time-lucky. He entered the dry sauna because of me. I'd been sitting there naked and he'd seen me through the window in the door. (Although I can't be sure of that; maybe he was planning to come in anyway). He had tiny scars on his face, pockmarks, though it's hard to be precise about that kind of thing when I'm not wearing my glasses. He positioned himself at the opposite end of the sauna, a couple of meters away from me, and leaned against the wall, his body taut and muscled, a white towel around his waist.

Earlier that morning, I'd seen men like him hanging on the walls of the Palais des Beaux Arts: Ribot's *St. Vincent* amongst crows and a wolf, the saint's muscular body the sole source of light in the painting, thin brushstrokes of black in the center of his cream-colored chest, his red nipples, and Achilles in Bastien-Lepage's *Priam aux pieds d'Achille*—the two men's fingers touching, Priam distressed, old and ragged, and Achilles upright in a loincloth, a gold chain around his ankle.

Number Three glared at the wall opposite him and at me on the wooden slats staring back at the outline of his cock against his towel. At that moment, I was every gay boy who has ever gazed at the locker room demigods, undeserving, yet unwavering in our devotion. And I thought, even if nothing happens between us, I have been this close, this alone in a room with a man whose beauty is pornographic in its splendor. Sometimes it's enough to be a witness. I do not masturbate to pornography, but I did masturbate in the presence of Number Three.

And then someone walked in.

Not all interruptions are a bad thing.

This interruption was a bad thing.

A tall young guy, so young he still had puppy fat, sits down and runs his hands through his hair and rests his elbows on his knees and sighs a very deep sigh, "Oh"—to let us know he is old enough to be jaded—"Let's face it, all this is a considerable effort, but I will endure for the greater good." He is awkward and harmless and he's detracting from the pornographic scenario we'd been working on. So I left. And I turned at the door to look at Number Three, who was not yet Number Three, just the Beautiful Thug, and our eyes met.

I would get what I wanted.

I love these places.

If Number Three had been Number Two, the dark enthusiast from twenty minutes ago, he'd have followed *tout de suite*. With Number Two there'd been no need to test anything. He and I had stayed in the steam room. We never went anywhere. (I rarely do.) At some point we'd stood under cold water and his cock had stayed hard, further proof of his keenness. The water had been like a tunnel of pure light in the dark, a beacon, a spotlight, an oasis of cool in the thick heat of the steam room, where I was now sitting and waiting for Number Three.

Waiting is not always an aphrodisiac. It belittles. Waiting can be a demeaning experience. It is evidence of powerlessness. Waiting for Number Three was none of these. I had time to imagine the curves of his chest and their firmness, the smoothness of his skin, the weight of his cock in my mouth and its saltiness. Waiting is part of hunting; it heightens the pleasure and fuels the imagination. Other types of waiting damage the soul; they lead to despair and loss of hope. Waiting for money, recognition, discovery, rescue—these are types of waiting I have known.

But I do not give up easily.

"No" is not something I like to take for an answer.

I went back to the dry sauna.

In my absence, Number Three had moved from one end of the sauna to the other, and was leaning against the wall beside the bench I'd been sitting on. The heat was intense. I took up the same position—picked up where I'd left off—and resumed playing with my cock. I stared at his body—his flat stomach, his hidden belly-button, his smooth tanned skin, his erect nipples—and confronted the menacing look that still intimidated me, built up the courage to lean over, like this, cautiously, to touch him.

At first I thought, he's going to hit me. He hates himself and hates his sexuality—he's a builder, a plumber, a garbage-collec-tor—and he's full of contempt for the *pédés* of this world. He is here to show his disgust. I was not about to back off; I would make fear my aphrodisiac. All the things that stifle and undermine me—fear, indifference, waiting—would keep me hard.

I touched him the way you touch something rarely found in na-ture. I touched him the way you touch a sacred object. I touched him gently, tentatively, because I thought, if this is all I get, at least I will carry it in my fingertips, this memory of the velvet flesh, the steel of his muscle. I will remember the awe—and hyperbole—his body inspired in me. I will forget nothing about his body.

When I tried to unclasp his towel, Number Three left the sauna room and made sure I followed. We turned right, then round the corner, up the stairs, and into the first cubicle on the left. Only then, facing each other, did I notice how short he was. Number Three was the shortest of the lot. He was also the most beautiful. I treated him like a porn star. I don't believe he expected anything less.

Number Three wanted to be fucked—I could tell from the way he spread his towel on the thin vinyl mattress, then lay back and offered his arse. But I'm no good at fucking in saunas, and definitely not after two hours of sweating and cold showers and fiddling around with Number One and Number Two. I'm sure there are men whose ability and desire to fuck would be heightened by these factors and by the fact that Number Three was quick to lie back, raise his legs in the air, and expose his arsehole. I am not like most men I know. I have very specific issues. Many of them have to do with waiting.

Number Three was not interested in conversation.

He had an arsehole that needed licking.

This licking of arseholes is something the French seem to like very much. (I am basing this statement on one afternoon at the sauna in Lille.) On all six video screens around the place, showing just as many porn movies, there was at some point a scene with a) rimming, or b) a close-up of someone's arsehole with someone playing with it. Kissing is not a priority, not in a culture where it happens with every arrival and departure. In England, where casual physical contact is so rare, no man has ever turned his head when I wanted to kiss him. Kissing in England is rarely refused. (I know people who would disagree with this.)

Number Three came while I licked his balls and fingered his arsehole, his cum arcing onto his stomach. I wanted to lick it up, to catch it on my tongue; it seemed the right thing to do. I thought of my lover back home, and I thought how easy it is to take risks, and how easy it is not to. I stayed on my knees jerking myself off, pressing my nipple against his thigh, and while he played with his cock—still thick and hard in its gold cock-ring—I came on the floor beneath the banquette.

I kissed his stomach, spread his cum across his torso, rubbed it in with his sweat. He had bristles in the concave between his nipples. The rest of his body was smooth, his legs, his thighs, everything. His cock was still hard in his fist.

"*Encore?*" I said.

"*Non*," he said.

He might have smiled at this point, but I cannot be sure.

"What's your name?" I said.

"*Quoi?*"

"*Comment tu t'appelle?*" I said.

I thought he might ask for mine in return.

But that was all Stefan said. Three words. And I said, *merci*. He smirked when I said that. I did not have my glasses on, so I could be mistaken; it might have been a smile.

If this had been London, if this had been the city I've made my home, I'd have initiated a conversation, kept flirting with Number Three, complimented him on his body, on the way he massaged my shoulders for just a few second while I sucked his cock. But my poor vocabulary makes me reticent, forces me to hold back, turns me silent. When he left, I stayed in the cubicle and lay on the thin mattress on the banquette. I thought about the dream I'd woken from that morning. In it I'd watched a man get beaten up by another man. The attacker had ordered his Rottweiler to bite the victim's hands and keep them behind his back so that the attacker could punch the man in the face. The victim's boyfriend looked on, I shouted "Police, police!" and even though there was a squad car parked outside the Chinese restaurant, no one came to help.

I remember waking up thinking that I was the victim, the boyfriend, the thug, the Rottweiler, and the absent policeman. It's a Gestaltian approach to dreaming. It's not often that I remember my dreams, which made me think that perhaps the dream was a foreshadowing of something, too. For a while I thought that Number Three was going to punch me, that I was going to be the cowardly boyfriend and the Rottweiler who made it all possible. I wouldn't have fought back. (I rarely do.)

Later, sitting in the bar area drinking Schweppes Limon, I watched two soldiers capture a young man at gunpoint and make him strip. One of the soldiers used his own substantial cock to slap the prisoner's face, and then made him suck it. The guns were M16 rifles. The bartender asked me if I'd been out that day, that it looked as though I'd caught some sun. I told him I'd been at the art gallery that morning, then I'd had lunch in a café on Place de Béthune. The lemonade was cool and sweet as it made its way down my gullet. The second soldier took his cock out of his trousers and inserted it into the prisoner's arse. Behind them was a bombed-out stone building with clusters of grass sprouting from the cracks in its wall. I spotted Number One again; he was heading for the Jacuzzi, and we locked eyes. I nodded, and from where I was sitting, even though I was not wearing my glasses, I was sure he nodded back.

—*La Lokal, Lille, Friday, 25 August, 2006*

Muscle Electric

Steven Bereznai

A naked man is lying on the floor in front of me. I'm stroking his cock.

"Harder," he says.

I comply.

He's lanky, like me, but shorter, with wisps of hair around his nipples and a patch on his pale lower belly. I went to electrolysis a few days ago so my fake-and-bake skin is deliciously smooth.

"Do the fire-starter stroke," he orders.

I flip through the card catalog of my memory and pull out the appropriate file, complete with diagram and written instructions. Like a Boy Scout, I twirl his dick between my palms, trying to create enough friction to ignite the kindling below.

"More lube," he says with his Adolf accent.

I think two things:

  1) Aren't you a bossy little German?

  2) What am I doing here?

I look around, unable to hide the doubt on my face. We're in a fluorescently lit conference room in the basement of a Toronto hotel. Chairs have been stacked and pushed against the wall. On the floor are half a dozen naked duos like our own. In each pairing, one man is lying atop a towel—a thin separation from the stained industrial carpet—and the second man is working the first man's dick with a variety of strokes we've been taught today, ranging from "The Rake," which involves the fingernails, to "The Twist and Shout," which is like wringing out a towel.

At thirty-one I'm the youngest here. The two naked guys to our left are in their fifties. One of them works out, but needs to watch his carbs. The other looks like he's never seen a gym in his life. Or the sun. Or a doctor to remove the moles scattered on his body.

"By the end of the weekend you will have massaged everybody else in this room," the course facilitator tells us.

I can do this.

I have to.

Because I can't keep going the way I have.

The crisis point: I'm at Fly, Toronto's gay dance mecca, home to the hottest of the hot, the flamboyantly shirtless, the carefully plucked.

Tonight I am a lone wolf. No wingman. No posse. I stand in the middle of the dance floor, lasers overhead, smoke rising around my ankles, go-go boys gyrating on their platforms. I mouth the words to Madonna's "Beautiful Stranger." I think of the music video that goes with the song, Madge gyrating her ass against Mike Myers' cheek, him dolled up as Austin Powers, International Man of Mystery, driving a convertible Shaguar.

Tonight's my night, I think, until I look around.

Over there is the scrawny guy from the florist shop who I turned down for a date months ago. And there, by the bar, buying a Rev, a blond stud I've lusted after for eons, who refuses to make eye contact with me. Then I see Doug, who kicked me out of bed in the middle of a one-night stand, and Roger, who I kicked out of bed under similar circumstances. I am surrounded by the ghosts of cruisings past—stark reminders of a love life that has failed to live up to the stories of friends, porn, and Edmund White. They avoid looking at me. I avoid looking at them. My former elation morphs into something dark, squeezing my chest.

I am not loved.

I could collapse from dehydration, I think, and there's not a single person here who'd bother to spit in my mouth as they stepped over my twitching body.

And that's when I see him. He's got the body of an Adonis and the face of a Portuguese angel. He gave me a free ginger ale once, back when he was still a bartender. He smiled. I ran away immediately, my stomach a tight knot. It took me months of stalking to figure out his work schedule, and to finally work up the courage to ask him out. It was during a quiet afternoon shift. He stood bored behind the bar.

Do it, I ordered myself.

"So, we should go on a date some time," I said, after ordering a ginger ale.

He smiled awkwardly.

"I'm seeing someone," he replied. I could tell it was a line that pained him to say, but which he'd said before, many times.

The soda pop cost me $2.50 and my pride.

I snap out of the memory. Around me people are thrashing on the dance floor. Madonna's been supplanted by Beyoncé. Amidst the rapture of tweaking club boys, my body turns to lead.

The Portuguese man of my dreams is passing me by. He pulls his boyfriend in tow.

So that's him, I note.

The guy's cute. I'm cuter. There, I said it.

"Hey," my Portuguese slice of heaven says to me.

I nod, my heart hammering, mouth dry, mind ablaze.

The boyfriend makes eye contact with me. He smiles. He offers me his bottle of water. My instinct is to slap it away. And then I remember what I thought moments ago, about collapsing from dehydration and no one caring enough to spit in my mouth as they stepped over me, and here is this stranger offering me a drink of water.

When you ask something of the universe and it gives it to you, you take it.

I barely taste the water on my lips, and I hand the bottle back.

Home alone that night, I sign up for the next Body Electric course to be held in Toronto.

The naked workshop, as I like to call it, doesn't begin—or end—with cock stroking.

"We are all sacred beings," our facilitator tells us. He's a burly man with a mustache and a soothing voice. "It's easy to say that, and easy to forget, especially in the hurly-burly of daily life."

And nightly gay life, I think.

"Let's break into pairs," the facilitator tells us.

I sit on the floor across from a pudgy man who rests on a pillow because of his scoliosis.

"What's something you like about your own body?" the facilitator asks.

"My arms," I tell my partner.

"My lips," my partner replies. "I love to kiss."

"What's something you like about the body of the man across from you?" the facilitator asks.

"Your eyes," I say, staring into them. They are a beautifully pale shade of brown.

"Your arms," he winks, and I smile back.

"Now take a deep breath," the facilitator tells us, "release, and switch partners."

I move left, he moves right.

"When we look at a person, often we think that what we see is what we get," the facilitator says, "but we all come from somewhere. We all have a history. We all have tribes. Those things are all a part of who we are. Tell the man across from you where you come from."

A bald, sagging man stares at me through his bifocals. "I was married up until two years ago, to a woman. She left me when I came out. I'm now sixty. She took the house. I'm in a tiny condo, and I am so grateful to be here right now."

My turn.

"My parents both escaped Hungary in the revolution of 1956," I say. "My dad was fifteen. He snuck across the border into Austria in the middle of the night, all by himself. My mom was with her family. They were in a large crate with two other families, and loaded onto a ship to get them out. They met in a Hungarian church here in Canada."

"Take a deep breath and release," our facilitator says. "Now find a new partner."

There is more sharing. More changing of partners. Turns out the German is straight and comes to these things to bond with men and "share" male energy. His girlfriend is cool with it. It's all very European. A friend of a friend is there, and we both blush a little as we sit naked on our towels across from each other. A guy with curly clown hair receding in the middle asks me if I want to meet up later, even though we've specifically been told not to be on-the-make.

"Take a deep breath," our facilitator says.

I release and find a new partner.

At the end of the day, the facilitator says in his hypnotic tones, "You've all done really well. This isn't an easy thing to do. Some of you may find yourselves thinking of not coming back tomorrow, but I should tell you something. Today you did eighty percent of the work, with only twenty percent of the benefit. Tomorrow is the opposite. It'll be twenty percent of the work, with eighty percent of the benefit. I look forward to seeing you all in the morning."

I retreat to my condo for the evening. In my rabbit box of stainless steel appliances, granite counter tops, and floor to ceiling windows, I flip through a *Muscle & Fitness* magazine. The issue is twenty years old, August of 1985. I was twelve when I bought it, feeding my obsession with the built boys within its pages, back before I realized this was a sexual attraction, and that this would soon become fodder for many masturbation sessions to come.

On the cover is former Mr. Universe, Bob Paris. He always prided himself on his proportionate body, and it is a beauty to behold in all its tanned and toned wonder. There's a gorgeous vein popping out on his clenched bicep. His posing trunk is pastel blue. His face is boyishly handsome, capped with curly brown hair. I shit bricks when he came out. I thought, that's the guy I want. Or at least that's the kind of guy I want. Muscular, handsome, young.

A bit out of my league, though. It didn't take long to realize most muscle guys go for other muscle guys. So I worked out and went on diet after diet. My body got better, but only up to a point. I never did reach cover model status.

I stare at Bob Paris and think, I don't want to be alone and sexually frustrated for the rest of my life.

The facilitator turns off the fluorescent lights and sets candles around the rented hotel conference room. There's a washroom out in the hall, but since we're all naked there's a bucket behind a makeshift curtain, with a lid to contain the odor.

It's day two.

Massage tables are set up in a circle in the middle of the room. We "erotically undress," which is a fancy way of saying we take our time stripping one another, then we hold hands in a circle, exchange hugs, and do some power breathing.

And then it's time.

"For the rest of the morning half of you will give massages while the other half of you will receive," our baritone facilitator explains. "In the afternoon, you'll switch it up. For those of you who are giving the massages, after ten minutes, I'll let you know that it's time to switch, and you'll move in a clockwise direction to start massaging the person on the next table over. After another ten minutes, you'll switch again. The point is to work around any desire you might have to work on one particular person over another. There's nothing wrong with that, but it's not what we're doing here today. Also, the people who are receiving the massages will be blindfolded, for much the same reason. This is about touch, not who is touching you."

A blindfold is pulled tight about my eyes, and I lie down under a sheet. The drumming begins. Warm oil is applied to my exposed chest. We're given breathing exercises. Slow, then fast, deep, then short, always in tempo to the changing rhythm of the drum. Incense is burned to mask the inevitable flatulence of bodies relaxing about the room.

More drumming. Massagers come and go every ten minutes, stroking my arms, chest, scrotum, and cock. I'm not hard, but I'm not totally soft either. More quick and shallow breaths, the beat of the drum growing frenzied. I'm relaxed and sweating at the same time.

The drums are slowing. They have stopped.

My hands and feet curl into claws against my will, my calves and forearms tightening. I'm later told this is because my breathing was off, that I was holding in more carbon dioxide than I was expelling. It creates a state sometimes intentionally induced as part of rebirth ceremonies.

I can see why. I start to trance out.

"Place the sheet over the body, covering the face," I hear from a long way off.

What I start to experience feels real the way a dream feels real. I am a Ken Doll. I really am. I'm in my toy packaging, a box that is my coffin. The sheet over me is tissue paper, encasing my Ken Doll body. I'm suffocating. Finally, the sheet is pulled off my body, and merciful air rushes in. I can breathe! But more than that, it's as if I'm being unwrapped, like a gift on Christmas, revealing me to the world. The box that is my coffin folds away.

Light and warmth shine in.

I am reborn.

At the end of the day we sit in a circle once more. We share and release one last breath. We dress. Safe within my underwear and jeans, I find they chafe ever so slightly. The guy with the curly clown hair comes up to me.

"So," he says, "we should meet up sometime to exchange massages. What's your number?"

"Uh, how about I get yours," I say.

He hands me his digits and stares at me awkwardly. The guy with scoliosis comes to my rescue.

"I'll walk you out," he says, putting his arm around me and leading me away.

"Thanks," I say.

"No problem," he replies. "You know, I think what I've learned from this weekend is that I can be erotic with just about anyone. But that curly haired dude is just creepy."

Underneath my laughter, I ponder his words.

I guess a guy doesn't have to be a muscle wet dream for me to be erotic with him. But could I have sex with the guys here? Not so sure.

My arm is around him. It feels comfortable and without charge, not the sexual kind, anyway. I guess that answers that question. Still, it feels nice. It is good to have this physical closeness with this man.

"So if you're ever in Detroit, let me know," he says.

Outside he hails a cab to take him to the airport.

"And if you're ever back in Toronto, let me know," I reply.

The cab pulls over.

We hug and share a friendly kiss.

"So did you get what you were looking for out of the weekend?"

I smirk playfully.

"It's a start."

Confessions of an Underground Wrestler

Tony Correia

"Your legs are seven times stronger than your arms," said the announcer, in a voice both nasal and authoritative. "Can you imagine the force and the strength being used to squeeze the air out of Tom Zenk right now?"

Zenk's white boots kicked the ring apron, pain gnarling his *GQ* looks, as he tried to extricate himself from between Nick Bockwinkel's thighs. Bockwinkel was hubris personified. He sat back on his hands, his black trunks pressed against the small of Zenk's back, not a hair on his blond head or chest out of place.

I was lying on my stomach, as close to the TV as I could get. My pubescent erection was practically levitating me off the floor, my cock harder each time the wresters bested each other. Instinctively, I rocked on my boner, pressing harder into the carpet.

After some choking and hair pulling by Bockwinkel, Zenk came back on the offensive. Whipping Bockwinkel into the ropes, Zenk launched himself and his red trunks and white boots into the air for a drop kick. Veteran that he was, Bockwinkel anticipated the move and hung onto the top rope. "No target there! No target there!" said the announcer, allegedly caught by surprise. Bockwinkel picked the prone Zenk up by the hair, draped him over the bottom rope, and dropped a knee across his back. Then he dragged Zenk back to the middle of the ring and finished him off by pile driving his head into the canvas.

As the referee's hand slapped three, it was as if my dick had broken in two. I rolled onto my back, panting, panicking, wondering how I was going to explain this to my geriatric parents—or to a doctor. "How did this happen?" my mother would ask in broken English.

"I was watching wrestling," I would stammer, "and it just exploded!"

I was afraid to look down, sure there was a pool of blood spreading through my pants. I prepared myself for the bright light that would come take my soul into the afterlife. Five minutes passed before I convinced myself I would see another tomorrow.

Had I pissed myself? I didn't smell urine. I stuck a hand down my pants to see. The yolky substance was neither piss nor blood. I smelled it, tasted it. Then every dirty word that I had ever heard at recess came back to me: Fuck, Cock, Cunt, Cum.

Oh my God, I thought, I was masturbating and I didn't even know it. There's a Catholic education for you.

From that Saturday on I was glued to the television noon to three, cheering on a Rougeau, a Putski, or a Bravo with each stroke of my cock. I wasn't fazed by the fact that I was masturbating to the sight of men—it was the action I was getting off on, I told myself, not the wrestlers. I was thirteen years old—this too would pass. If my family noticed anything strange, they didn't mention it. Then again, wrestling and hockey were staple viewing in our household; my parents didn't need to speak English to understand what was going on.

I always felt I missed my calling as a professional wrestler. While my classmates were touring university campuses, I was looking up the number of pro wrestling schools in the Yellow Pages or dreaming of running away and training with Gene Kiniski in Vancouver. The only thing stopping me was my family; what would they think? This dream will fade, I tried to console myself, just like my homosexuality. Otherwise, both were my little secrets. Missed opportunities or not, those years of watching wrestling and masturbating defined me sexually.

Eighteen years later I discovered I was not alone, and that dreams, like myths, never die.

"This is not what I imagined when you said you had a ring," I said, my voice echoing in the cold and mildew-scented air.

Yellow nylon ropes were stretched across the width of a storage room in a Tenderloin basement. Gym mats covered the cement floor in clumps; posters for wrestling cards in small American towns decorated the walls. For all I knew, there were people buried under the floor.

I met Trout in a wrestling chat room on AOL. Every day, as soon as I logged onto my computer, an Instant Message would pop up from him. "So when are we going to wrestle, stud?" he would ask. I could almost hear him panting.

Trout was in his fifties and had been doing some kind of fighting in private for more than twenty years. In his photo he was Gollum-like. Evidence to the contrary, he insisted on describing himself as "muscular." I finally took him up on his offer, not just to get him off my back, but also to get the wrestling thing out of my system.

"I'm a good teacher," he insisted. He seemed sincere. And he had a ring.

"So, do you get many matches?" I asked, pulling my Speedos and wrestling shoes out of my gym bag.

"It's hit or miss," he said in a cigar-strained voice. "I do a lot of traveling. AOL has made it a whole lot easier. You used to have to subscribe to Joe Gillespie."

"Who's that?"

"He published a wrestling newsletter that came out of the New York Wrestling Club once a month. Sometimes there was a pic with an ad, but guys mostly just described themselves and how to reach them." Trout struggled with the laces of his professional wrestling boots, missing a hole, and started again. "It was a pain in the ass. You had to exchange photos by mail—no JPEGS, no instant messages. It took weeks to hear back from someone, and you were lucky if you got a pic of anyone in wrestling gear."

"What about the phone?"

"Long distance rates weren't what they are now," he grunted, tightening his bootlaces. "But people weren't so picky—they were desperate to wrestle and there were so few of us, not like now."

There were goose bumps on my legs as I stretched on the cold mats. I found myself caught up in the romance of Joe Gillespie and the Herculean efforts of his disciples as they wrestled their way across North America and around the world. It was reassuring to know that the realm I was entering was no mere fetish, but the stuff of legend.

I stood in the middle of the ring, shivering. Trout danced from toe to toe in the corner. "Ready?" he asked.

"Ready as I'll ever be."

We locked up. Trout put me in a headlock and hip tossed me onto the mat. What followed was a succession of scissors, punches, chokes, and arm bars. With each new hold I kept expecting Trout to stop and explain what it was he was doing. When he hung onto a chokehold after I submitted, it was time to go home.

"I thought you were going to explain the moves," I said, throwing my sweaty Speedos into my bag.

"I showed them on you. You learn by doing."

Trout was waiting for me online when I got home. "That was a great match, stud," he said. "When can we do it again?" I strung him along for a few weeks, making excuses, sparing his feelings, until he called me a "pretty boy fascist" and told me to fuck myself. With Trout behind me, so was the physical manifestation of my heart's desires.

Sometimes it seems there's a civic holiday in San Francisco for every fetish except wrestling. You can piss on a guy, fist-fuck him, lash him to an inverted cross, whip his back, or just jack him off. But tell him you want to wrestle and he thinks you're weird. And as with other fetishes, there are sub-categories. Some guys are only into submission with stakes. Others are solely into gut punching. I always steered clear of guys who wanted to get knocked unconscious. Even with a set of criteria, you had to weed out the fakes.

My first real breakthrough came when "Cujo" responded to my personal ad on Rec Pro Wrestling. "Into long submission matches in Speedos and bare feet. LTR," his email read, followed by his stats: five-eight, one hundred eighty pounds. Included in the email was a picture of him posing in a pair of square cut trunks on a wrestling mat.

Wrestlers are never as intimidating at your front door as they are in the pictures they email and post. Cujo looked small and bookish, not at all like the gnarled brute in his photo. Both of us were wearing glasses; we greeted each other like visiting dignitaries. The bed frame was already leaning against the wall, the mattress and box spring side by side on the floor, when I showed him into the apartment. "Welcome to the Wrestletorium," I said.

"Wrestletorium," he snorted. "I like that." He dropped his gym bag on the floor and bent down to unzip it. "So how long have you been wrestling?" he asked.

"A couple of months. You're my fifth match."

"A newbie. I promise not to go gentle on you. Liking it so far?

"Put it this way: My first match was with Trout."

"Ugh! Trout," Cujo said. "I'll never make that mistake again."

"I ended my second match because my opponent tried to pile drive me. I have a no-pile-driver rule. The guy after that screamed like a girl when I put him in a headlock. My last opponent left after I stripped down to my boxer shorts."

"I've had that happen."

"Now I have to look at him at the gym and wonder if he's told everyone he knows."

"I think that would work to your advantage."

"What about you? How long have you been wrestling?"

"On and off, about ten years. I go through phases. Back in the days of Joe Gillespie, you took any match you could get, but now with the Internet, you can pick and choose. It's nice."

"What does your boyfriend think?"

"He gets into it sometimes. He likes to watch. He wanted to come tonight."

"Yeah, so you said in your last email. This is hard enough as it is without a cheering section."

Cujo rolled his neck and faced me, kneeling on the mattress. "Ready?"

"As I'll ever be …"

It was the first of many collar and elbow lock-ups. Cujo had the upper hand in sheer strength but was not an endurance wrestler— he smoked. He would take the first couple of rounds and then the real wrestling would begin. I would wait for him to get tired before launching my offensive, using sweat as lubricant to maneuver out of a hold. It was hard submit to him; I did so only a handful of times.

We wrestled about once a month. Before every match we caught up on our lives, conventional and wrestling. There were matches where we talked more than wrestled, lying in our Speedos, our sweaty chests and stomachs heaving from our efforts, his calf across my shin, trying to solve the world's problems and our own.

"Wrestle for stakes? Best two out of three?" he asked out of the blue.

"Sure," I said. In the six months that we had been wrestling partners, we had never so much as kissed. "What about your boyfriend?"

"Don't worry about my boyfriend."

Cujo was more aggressive than usual. He took me in two quick falls. He rolled me over onto my stomach, ripped my Speedos off, and shoved his cock up my ass as soon as he could get a condom over it. It was the best fuck ever. Cujo collapsed on my back, panting in my ear. The panting became whimpering.

"Dude … what are you crying for? You won!"

"My boyfriend left me for another man," he said, wiping his tears on the back of my neck.

As the name suggested, the Badlands was barren and empty. As the new bartender, I kept myself busy polishing bottles until Happy Hour started. To pass the time, I re-read the license plates screwed into the wall. There were hundreds of them, each with an anagram for sex. Where there wasn't a license plate, there were horns, portraits of Indian Chiefs, spurs, saddles, and lots of wood to sit and lean on. It was a bar born out of childhood fantasies of John Wayne, *Bonanza*, and *Gunsmoke*, the kind of place you kept expecting tumbleweed to blow through.

The sunlight coming in the swinging doors blinded me. I tried not to look too anxious as I watched a silhouette enter the bar and take a stool. "I'll 'ave a pint of Bud," said a thick British accent. Suddenly, I was on *Coronation Street*.

"Are you Fullnelsn?" the man asked as I poured him his beer.

I blushed. "That's a name I don't normally answer to outside of the Internet."

"They said I would find you here."

"Who's they?"

"Some blokes I've been chatting with online. Nice pic."

"And who are you?"

"Pro/SubUK."

"Doesn't ring any bells."

"I'm not on AOL, but I'm listed on *Vangar* and *Takedown*."

We sized each other up, approximating weight and strength, both of us telling ourselves, I can take him. There was a pause in the conversation similar to the kind in a match, where you're just resting and breathing, waiting to see what your opponent is going to do next.

"I hear you've a mat."

"Yeah. I got sick of stopping a match to push the mattress and bedspring together."

The mat was eight by eight, a couple of inches thick. There were small thumb-sized gauges in the blue rubber, and it smelled a bit rank, but it was sturdier than any mattress. I found it refurbished online from a place in Richmond, BC. It had been turned back at the border once before it arrived on my doorstep. A procession of neighbors helped me carry it into my apartment, not batting an eye.

"You wanna wrestle?" It was as if Pro/SubUK had crossed the ocean and the continent specifically to issue the challenge, like a character out of a spaghetti western. Throw a poncho on him, shove a toothpick into the side of his mouth, and as long as he didn't talk, he was Clint Eastwood. How could I refuse?

"You're on. Tomorrow. Noon. My place," I said, writing out directions from the bar. "So how long have you been in the States?"

"Three weeks. I was in Boston 'til a week ago. Came to San Fran with the money I made for doing a BG video."

"You did a wrestling video? Pro or sub?"

"Bit of both. Made a fool of myself, I'm sure."

"You're probably being too hard on yourself."

"I wish I could burn the tape."

"But you're famous now. In these circles you're a wrestling god. When you least expect it, someone will stop and tell you how they got off watching you wrestle."

"Or someone could play it at a party."

"There's that, too." There was no convincing him otherwise, he was doomed to live down his wrestling video like a bad tattoo. "So … wrestling anyone else while you're here?"

"Bloke named Trout. Says he has a ring. Heard of him?"

The match was not nearly as exciting as our conversation. Pro/Sub-UK was raised on British pro wrestling that is more choreographed and polite compared to the guerilla tactics of North American wrestling. Our styles didn't gel. "Do you fancy this?" he asked between falls.

"Yes," I lied.

The match lasted barely an hour, ending in a draw. Many years later someone gave me the video Pro/SubUK had filmed for BG East. I'm not sure if I made him nervous or the camera freed him of inhibitions, but if we'd had the match that he taped, I would have married him.

Jocko couldn't have been more All-American if he walked around in a letterman sweater eating apple pie. He was straight, married, and really into pro wrestling. When we crossed paths, he was un-employed and I was working three days a week. The topic of his wife and family were strictly taboo. Wrestling was the only thing we had in common.

"The ring has a great bounce to it," Jocko said. "There are tires under the ring apron. It's like wrestling on a springboard."

"Those aren't on, are they?" I asked, pointing at the video cam-eras aimed at the ring. The ring belonged to a friend of Jocko's who was taking a stab at the wrestling video industry, a venture financed with dot.com money. It was in a warehouse under the Bay Bridge. The ring was brand new, the grey mats shining in the spotlight.

"No. But I'll double check anyway."

My hands were shaking as I changed into my gear. I climbed up the apron and pulled hard on the ropes. The ring posts didn't budge. I stepped through and took a deep breath. Jocko turned off all the lights except for the spotlight above the ring. I felt like I was in Madison Square Gardens, the crowd invisible to me in the dark.

I grabbed a handful of Jocko's hair as he was climbing through the ropes, helping him into the ring. I rammed his head into the turnbuckle a couple of times until he blocked it, spun me around, and whipped me across the ring into the opposite corner. It was like falling off a cliff and landing in a snow bank. We wrestled like that for about an hour, back and forth, give and take, going for the pin, and kicking out on the two count.

Jocko was sitting on my chest, pretending to choke me. I kicked the mat with my boots, shaking my head back and forth, my hands on his wrists. Jocko's head and shoulders eclipsed the spotlight, his blond hair a halo around his head. There, in the umbra of Jocko's face, emanated Nick Bockwinkel's Roman nose, bushy brow, and arrogant smile.

"What's wrong?" Jocko asked, loosening his grip.

"Don't talk, keep choking me," I gasped, keeping up the charade. "I want you to give me a pile driver and pin me."

"What happened to no pile drivers?"

"Don't talk, just do."

Jocko picked me up by the hair and threw me against the ropes, meeting me with a boot to the stomach. He pushed my head between his thighs and sat down hard on the mat, taking me with him. My skull came nowhere near the mat, but I rolled over on my back, annihilated. I beamed back up at the spotlight as Jocko covered me and hooked my leg for the count of three. At long last, I had come home.

I fulfilled my dream of going to a pro wrestling school when I moved back to Vancouver. It was compensation for moving to a city with a small wrestling population—and it looks good on my profile. I learned how to run the ropes, take bumps, and shape the structure of a match. "Remember," the coach would yell, "you're telling a story!" But the wrestling I knew and loved was nothing like the wrestling my colleagues had grown up watching. Where there were once suplexes, there were now moonsaults; matches didn't end with a pin or submission, but devastation and humiliation. This was a dream whose time had come.

But to this day, nothing turns me on more than a man in pro wrestling gear. Every morning before work, I'll log onto the wrestling websites looking for photos of men in pro trunks and boots, mimicking stances from old wrestling magazines, condos and basements standing in for arenas and TV studios. Like me, they're clinging to the memories of an innocent time when wrestling was a carnival, not a corporation—preserving those memories—just like Joe Gillespie before us.

Connecting

K.P. Lukoff

That weekend, he called me "boy" as if it were my name.

We had just become friends. Kevin was an older transsexual who had started to transition when I had been in the second grade. I met him at a leather contest. When I ran into him a few months later at another leather event, we exchanged email addresses. I hung out with him and his partner one weekend and fell hopelessly in love, like a puppy chasing a truck.

I came out as transgender, female-to-male, when I was twenty, and started playing with BDSM around the same time. Most of my friends in the scene were straight or dykes, but after a few years I fell in with a gay men's leather crowd. Still, it was tough being a young transboy surrounded by gay men. They often didn't know what to make of me. When I met Kevin, I swooned. Not only was he tall, dark, and handsome, well-known in the leather community, and a self-proclaimed Top, I figured he was unlikely to have any problems with my pre-surgery body. The rational part of my brain swore that I wouldn't get my hopes up—he lived in a different state, was in a (non-monogamous) relationship, and didn't seem to have time in his life for a steady boy.

Still, I was excited. One weekend in April, about a month after I fell for him, we ended up in San Francisco for the same leather conference. In an uncharacteristic display of courage, I asked him if I could crash on his hotel floor, being young and broke. He told me he was staying with his old friend Franklin, but I was welcome to stay there as well.

He arrived late Friday night, missing the opening speech. He was in the lobby when I left and was talking to a friend, another older transman, Jason. There was a gathering in the hospitality suite upstairs, with chips and chicken wings, so we and most of the other attendees went up there.

I got over my fear of crowds and mingled, charming boy that I am. Then, while I was chatting with a fellow New Yorker I had a lingering crush on, Kevin reached over and started petting my head. I grinned and said to my friend, "This is why I keep my hair short." He said, with a mischievous smile, "For Kevin? Or just in general?" *Shut up!* I thought, *you're blowing my cover!* Kevin and Jason and Franklin decided to get dinner. I tagged along, and the New Yorker winked at me as we left.

After dinner, we went to Franklin's. We dropped off our stuff and prepared to go to the men's-only play party at a local SM club. I feigned nonchalance while Kevin and Jason perused Franklin's collection of whips and canes, which easily numbered more than a hundred. They picked out a few nasty looking implements, and, thus equipped, we set out into the night.

The party was quiet. The space was hushed, reverential, and there weren't many men—we were all disappointed by the low turnout. I was also out of my depth; I had never been to an exclusively male sex party before and wasn't accustomed to the atmosphere. I had figured we would split off, the two of them tricking with someone, and I would either get lucky with someone else or stand around awkwardly. But the three of us snagged a place to sit in the social area to watch a scene going on below. I again feigned nonchalance, looking around as Jason and Kevin talked quietly to each other.

Kevin turned to me. "The party's awfully quiet," he said. I nodded. "You want to make our own party?" I nodded again. He asked me where I liked to get hit, and how much clothing I'd be comfortable removing. With limits negotiated, we headed downstairs. I toyed with telling him how utterly terrified I was, but decided to pretend this sort of thing happened to me all the time.

I think this was my first time wearing restraints while getting beaten—a pair of beautiful leather cuffs that went around my wrists and hands, with space for the thumb, clipped to a bondage stand. It was also my first time getting co-topped. Definitely only the second or third time I'd played with someone I was infatuated with. It was also the first time that I was desperately uncomfortable taking off my binder, not having had chest surgery, but I worked up the courage to do so because they asked me to, swore up and down that none of the men would care, that they would have more fun if I did.

I've found it's much easier to take a heavy beating when someone else is standing in front of you, stroking you, talking to you. Or holding you and responding with affirmation when you express pain. Easier, almost, when two people are separately hurting two different parts of your body, making you recite what little you remember from law school about torts, assault, and negligent infliction.

It's harder when you have to keep your eyes shut tight to avoid looking at your body, when the occasional accidental downward glance makes your trussed-up arms convulse toward your chest. But it's made better when the two men tell you that they've been there before, they've felt how you feel, and it's okay, boy, you're doing a good job, boy. Calling you a brave boy, a good boy, a strong boy.

It was … intense isn't the word. After a good long while I was reaching the end of my endurance and said hesitantly to Kevin, warning him, "I think I might start to cry if you keep doing that."

A pause.

"Is that something you want, boy?" he asked then. "Is that somewhere you want me to take you?"

I couldn't answer truthfully, because there was no truthful answer.

He said, "All right. I'm going to give you ten more blows, and then I want to take you down. If you start to cry, that's okay. If you don't, that's okay too. How's that sound?"

I acquiesced, and was almost disappointed that only a tear or two gathered at the corners of my eyes.

When I'd first met Kevin, he made a disparaging comment about "aftercare," lumping it into a general category labeled "bullshit." I therefore figured he'd be another top who was just going to pat me on the shoulder and walk away when he was done. Mentally, I prepared myself for that outcome.

I was not prepared for being sandwiched between Kevin and Jason at the end, having Kevin breathe onto my neck or kiss me. Idiot that I am, I stammered a complete sentence or two. "Why are you doing this? You can stop! I thought, I mean, didn't you say you hate aftercare?"

"I do hate aftercare," he said.

"Well, but, I mean, what do you call this?"

"This? I don't know. It's just part of the scene."

I spent the next week excited, happy, and turned on because he had put his arm around my shoulders once or twice. I didn't know how to react when, the morning after that first intense scene, we woke up together and he said, "C'mere," tugging me toward him so my head was resting on his bare chest. He put his arms around me, asked how I slept, stroked my arms and back and head.

In direct opposition to everything my mind was telling me, the next week I asked if I could be his boy. I knew that all the odds were against me. But I felt a connection between us and knew that something had to come from it. After a vigorous back-and-forth, tough questions and tougher answers, Kevin accepted my request.

I no longer get to choose whether or not he makes me cry, and I wouldn't have it any other way.

First Touch

'Nathan Burgoine

In my youth, I moved often. I spent a great deal of my time alone, the "new kid." When I moved to a new place, I would explore in long, rambling walks, and try to find places I could enjoy on my own.

There is an island in the interior of British Columbia where an artist carved faces into the trees. The bridge to Zukerberg Island is unnerving, a narrow suspension that sways alarmingly. The artist built a tiny shack, which served as a stepping-stone domicile; he and his wife lived in the tiny space while building a larger cabin.

I lived near this island for my Grade Eleven and for the summer before school started. When I discovered it on one of my lonely rambles, there was no door on the smaller shack, though a plaque explained the history of both the shack and the cabin, which was now a museum that I, at age sixteen, had no intention of paying to enter. But I went to the little shack often, to read, to draw, or to scribble in my journal.

As a new kid, I was noticed for few things, but one was my ability to speak French; I was schooled in eastern Canada, where French instruction was more prominent, before heading west. And so a plan was hatched by my parents and a French teacher—I would tutor French comprehension and vocabulary.

This was how Erik and I met. Otherwise, we never would have. Erik was two years my elder and moved in the social circles of the athletic. He was not a shining academic. That we might have anything in common was unlikely. Erik was the iconic dream-come-true of parents: athletic and handsome, with unruly blond hair and a winning smile, enormously popular. I, on the other hand, was a faded version of a lesser ideal: slim, bookish (the only thing unruly about me was my slowly emerging sarcasm), and quiet.

We would meet twice a week; once at my home, once at his, and after school on some days would walk home together. I would aim French at him, and mostly miss.

Erik was casual with his touch. He roughhoused in the manner of athletes, grabbing me around the neck with one arm or punching my shoulder, even initiating mock wrestling battles I inevitably lost in the space of seconds. Before Erik, this was a form of touch I had never experienced, and I found myself flustered and confused, craving the contact and dreading what that meant.

During one of our "French walks," it rained. We were nearer the unnerving bridge than to either of our homes, and as I had taken refuge in the tiny cabin by myself during previous rains, I suggested we dash to it.

I am tall. Erik was not short. The result was that though one could stay dry inside the doorless shack, two could not—not without touching. I drew my feet up tightly, knees to my chest, to make room, but instead of using the remaining space, Erik used my legs as a backrest, craned his neck back over my knees, and looking at me upside-down, said, "You make a great chair."

I could see down the front of his T-shirt. His abundant chest hair was darker than his head of blond hair.

I put my arms over his shoulders, resting my forearms on either side of his head, and said, "You make a good arm rest."

We sat in silence, but for the rain.

I wanted that moment to last a long time. But I was rapidly losing sensation in my legs and elbows—and I had a growing discomfort of a different sort elsewhere. Eventually, I had to admit the former, if only to hide the latter.

"You're heavy," I said.

He sat forward, and while he had his back to me, I spread out my legs to either side of him while adjusting my real concern. Before

I was ready, he leaned back again, between my legs, with his head all but resting in my lap, looking up at me with a grin. Erik took my arms in his hands, and in a moment I will remember forever, crossed them over his chest, then closed his eyes.

His body's heat and soapy scent were so overwhelming that I began to tremble.

"You okay?" he asked, eyes still closed.

I managed, "Yes. No. Yes." Not eloquent.

He laughed, and opened his eyes. Unable to meet his gaze, I looked instead at his chest. I could see beneath the V of his shirt, to the curve of his muscled pecs. I shifted my right hand so my thumb rested under his neck.

I was hyperaware. I could feel his heartbeat, the warmth of his skin under his T-shirt along my arm, warmer on my thumb where I touched skin, not shirt, while my left hand rested lightly on his chest. My surging erection had to have been obvious.

I had never done anything like this with another boy. And yet, what were we doing? Erik was leaning on me. I was resting my arms on him. I had moved my thumb perhaps an inch. It was just touch. But touching had never felt like this.

"I ..." I started, but had no idea what to say after that. Trembling was giving way to shaking. I felt real fear. Erik grinned at me, but I shifted my eyes from his face.

My thumb moved: up, down. I stroked the hollow of his throat where it met his chest. When his arms, loose over mine, stayed put, I got braver. The circles I traced with my thumb grew wider in aching progression, until a finger joined the thumb on his skin. Then another. When my hand went under his shirt, his eyes closed again. He was smiling.

That he was athletic, I knew, and had seen, but to touch him—so different from the softness of a girl!—to feel his chest, the hairs rough against my right palm, was so masculine a sensation that I was as terrified as I was aroused. I couldn't stop, couldn't talk, and didn't want to move but for those lazy circles I traced with my right hand.

When he shifted, I froze, my hand now far enough down his shirt that it was caught in his motion, and came free with an awkward jerk. When he sat up and turned around and saw my face, he laughed for long enough that I managed to be both hurt and relieved in turn. My face was hot, I was confused, aroused—and completely lost, desperate to flee and desperate not to.

Erik leaned against the opposite wall of the shack and said, "Come here."

At first I was frozen to the spot, but he teased me past embarrassment. When I lay against him, the sensation of his touch, even through my shirt, jolted me. My fantasy of touch from another boy, another man, was a soul-shattering reality.

We crossed borders together. We opened our bodies to each other. I astounded myself by pulling off his shirt, by kissing and licking his torso. We didn't need words; they might have got in the way. Erik, more experienced, brought his lips to mine, and I learned that kissing a boy was even more thrilling than touching a boy. We caressed each other's cocks through underwear chosen that morning without forethought, and when I drew his cloth-sheathed cock into my mouth, our orgasms were inevitable, and immediate.

He rested against me after we came, both of us at ease. Soon after, we headed home in the rain, going our separate ways.

This experience left me breathless. I had no words then for our rubbing, our kissing, our release, and I shivered more from the memory than from the cold rain.

My mother fretted and tutted when she saw me, and weeks later—by which time Erik and I were spending as much time as we could in each other's company—I overheard her complain about "that older boy."

My father told her it was probably a good thing that we were hanging out so much. "Maybe," he said, "Erik will rub off on him."

When I passed my father's comment on to Erik a night or two

later, he happily obliged—though more physically than my father intended.

With time, after discussions that were at first awkward, our erotic encounters intensified, sex initiated with one of us saying, "Come here," Erik reaching to touch my chest, me reaching to touch his. Always that touch, the palm of my soft hand against his hairy, hard chest, his rough palm against my softer chest, slow, teasing circles before we tried to mimic the man-on-man positions depicted in Erik's skin magazines, often laughing at our attempts.

No matter how it ended, our sex always began with that promise of touch—masculine but loving, heavy with the promise of more touching to come—the sensual touch I carry with me even now, years later.

Just An Ordinary Weekend

Sky Gilbert

1. Me

Fifty-six, six feet tall, dark, big, shaved head, some piercings and tattoos. A writer. Hamilton, Ontario, Canada.

2. Modus Operandi

Weekend sex, mostly. Home base is a Toronto *pied-à-terre*. Don't bring people home because of agreement with boyfriend, though. Most of my pickups are at bars and baths. Hey, I'm old-fashioned. Don't like penetrative sex too much. I like to come (I've always been goal-oriented). I'm a Sagittarian.

3. What a Typical Weekend Entails

This weekend starts on Thursday. I go St Marc's Spa on Yonge Street. They're having an Asian night. Hey, I'm game. There's a guy lying on a massage table in the lobby with sushi all over him. I'm open-minded—but. I've always had a not-so-positive feeling about food and sex together, so I go straight to my room. Not much action for a while. Tum-te-dum. I sit on my bed and watch porn. I want to meet my friends at Woody's later so I'm anxious to get tonight's sex over with. Oh, there's a guy. He's handsome, but— how young is he—maybe thirty-ish? Very white—like he might be a businessman or something. Then he's in my room. He's still handsome. That's a good sign. My only complaint is his body isn't fabulous (though it's not bad), and when I touch his ass he clenches it really tight like "don't go in there!" (Not that I would necessarily go there, but what's the problem?) He's very appreciative of me; he starts to suck on my tits right away. I play with my cock. I notice when he's sucking me off that he looks really good when you look down on him, but when you look up at him from underneath he doesn't have much of a chin. (I notice this when he stands on the bed and demands I suck his not-too-spectacular cock.) I begin to get turned off and tell him I want a rest. He is about to leave, but kisses me and starts sucking on my tit again. There's something about his hand on my neck as he does that (and the fact that I want to get out of here) that makes me feel pressured and pushed around in just the right way. I come. So does he. It's over. Goodbye. On my way out of St Marc's the cute door guy says, "Aren't you going to stay and see the Live Sex Show?" I say, "I just had one in my room, but nobody came to see it!" He laughs really hard.

I'm on my way.

On Friday afternoon I go to another bathhouse (Spa Excess), and I've just arrived in my room when this really hot, exotic-looking guy walks past my door. (What is he? Aboriginal South American? Maybe ... who cares?) Beautiful body, hair on his chest. Into worshipping me. He sucks me off—Jesus, so expertly. I don't know what he's doing exactly, but he lets me get right down in there and he chokes on it. (Hey, I'm not that big—but flattery will get you everywhere!) When I look down at him he's jerking off a very big black cock. (How come some guys have white skin and black cocks?) I touch his tits now and then and he moans. I don't usually like getting sucked off, but this guy's tongue and mouth are so wet they make me forget everything and I shoot my load. He spits some out and wipes his mouth. I was making so much noise, for Chrisssakes, he must have known I was going to spew. Well, I think he did, 'cause he gives me a nice thank-you kiss goodbye.

That night, I start at Woody's, and I'm being sociable for a while. Then I go to my favorite (i.e., the only) leather bar, The Eagle. Straight to the back room. Very drunk. Nobody is the least bit interested. Jesus, what's the problem? I was hot before. There's this incredibly cute guy—slender, tall, young, handsome—but I know he's just into being the center of a group scene. Boring. I don't want to be one of the Five Thousand Fingers of Doctor T. I want a guy of my own, but not here, because I seem to be enormously unpopular.

I go back to Woody's, which is where I left my coat. Woody's is Toronto's Cheers. I am very drunk, and I stand with my shirt unzipped facing a mirrored wall. This guy stands in front of me. He's in his twenties and has a bit of facial hair and sexy brown eyes and a baseball cap. Yum. He is saying very flirty things to me with a Spanish accent. "Where is it hot to hang out now? Where should I go?" I try to be a nice tour guide; maybe after all he's not flirting, maybe he really does want to go somewhere else. So I tell him where he might get lucky. He does not leave. He stands looking at me with gorgeous, juicy, luscious eyes. It starts with kissing. I just had to kiss him. "What do you like to do?" he asks. I hate that question. "Suck and get sucked," I say, to show I'm reciprocal and also so he can fuck off if he is obsessed with putting dicks into asses, which, I repeat, is not normally my favorite thing. He doesn't fuck off. Instead he says, "I like that too." Looks like we have a point of departure, and I'm experiencing liftoff, which is not too common, as you might imagine, with someone my age. I suggest that we go to a dirty video store up the road.

We talk along the way. His name is Fernando, he's been here a month, he's from Mexico. I ask him about Puerto Vallarta where my partner and I are thinking of going on vacation. He recommends it. We stagger down the stairs into the dirty video place, buy our tokens, and get ourselves a cozy cubicle. He rips off his clothes. I notice that he is quite hairy and has a big dick—all very positive. We kiss and hug and hold onto each other for dear life, and I realize that he wants to leave the door open. Soon there's a crowd. Well, three guys—two watching and another one trying to get into the room. I know the one trying to get in. He's an attractive weirdo. Young, but with gray hair. I had sex with him once because he has a cute face, but he wouldn't let me kiss him, and didn't really want to be touched. I find him sexy, however, so I don't mind that he's right next to us jerking off. I go down on Fernando's oh-my-god-it-fits-perfectly-down-my-throat-uncut-dick-from-hell. I love being force-fed dicks like this, and I come on the floor and on me. The mess is all over my arm, and Fernando makes me eat it. A perfect capper to a fabulous evening. We kiss and say goodbye. Fernando might have stayed at the dirty video place and gotten it on with somebody else after, maybe one of the guys who was watching us. On my way up the stairs somebody stops me. "Are you Sky Gilbert?" he asks. "Yes," I say. "I find your work really inspiring." I thank him and say, "That means a lot." (It does.) But it's making me feel too much like Judy Garland. Time to go back to the *pied-à-terre* and sleep.

On Saturday, I still want a little more sex. So I go back to the Spa Excess in the afternoon. I don't find anyone attractive; in fact, it looks like an episode of Star Trek where you've landed on the Planet of the Uglies. Tum-te-dum. Oh, a cute guy. Cute guy keeps coming by. I show my dick. He seems to like it. He comes in. Oooh: up close he's all dark and curly and Italian with a perfect slender torso and hairy legs and a nice cock that's automatically hard. I try to give him a good suck job. But even though he's very appreciative I have a feeling he'd rather be somewhere else. I don't know how I know that, I just do. It's not like he doesn't like me—he just knows there might be better fun somewhere else. He excuses himself, nicely. No big deal. I've had enough sex for one weekend, I think.

Or have I?

Something about Muscle

Andy Quan

Gay men can be as competitive and nasty as any other sexuality and gender, but it takes its own form. A philosophy, in three parts. Men I hate: those who attract, with barely an effort, men whom they are attracted to themselves. Men I feel sorry for: those who cannot attract those whom they are attracted to themselves. Men who attract men they are not attracted to: run faster.

I generally feel sorry for myself, but pretend I don't, at least, I don't make it public. So, when I was changing out of my sweaty gym gear in the locker room of Urban Fitness and noticed in the corner of my vision what appeared to be a man looking at me, a man who seemed to have very big muscles, albeit on a short frame, I thought, "Nah. This doesn't happen to me." And when he looked again, and I was suddenly sure he was looking at me, even though I was too disarmed and nervous to meet his eyes, I remembered my philosophy and said to myself with a wry grin, "I hate you." I think he saw me smiling to myself, which was not a bad thing; without even trying, I had let him know that 1) I'd noticed his stare, and 2) I was very pleased with myself. Who cares that I was changing to go, and he was getting into his gear? I could figure it out!

When he left the change room before me, I wondered if I was going to have to find him among the maze of equipment and then make it look natural that I had something to say to him. But I didn't have to worry. He was waiting for me in the stairwell.

I won't bother recounting the introduction, because they're all the same. You can imagine it: greeting, returned greeting, innocuous question, maybe a comment, reply to said question-comment, volley, return-volley, and so forth. Match point. Game! This one ended quickly, easily, and successfully: useful information, good news, and a phone number.

The useful information was his name, Morgan, and his occupation, window-cleaner (I like to know what people do). The good news was that he lived a block away from me, and it sounded like arranging a meeting would be simple.

I walked home, still taking in his physical appearance. He was older than most men I looked at. A spiderweb of lines at the corners of his eyes. A settled ruggedness. His lips had an odd wrinkled fullness about them. His muscularity was sinewy, defined, and large. My glimpse of him in the changing room was of something I'd fantasized about. He'd spent time in the sun, maybe too much time—Aussies are prone to skin cancer—and his skin was a ruddy tan color. He was either the same height or shorter than me: 5' 8", I'd guess.

That night, I let his image fill my head. I jacked off, coming almost immediately.

I date my fascination with muscle to my childhood. I remember a documentary on Arnold Schwarzenegger called *Pumping Iron* and seeing various bodybuilding competitions on television. The best were the homegrown varieties. British Columbia's Provincial Championships, which I think I caught only twice, had close-up camera-work, and the men, in their variations from short to awfully big, seemed more real, their coloring more natural than the oily tans illuminated by the bright spotlights I remember from Mr. Olympia and Mr. America.

No one required me to say why these men attracted me, so I never questioned it. Just watched with amazement at the patterns made when different poses were flexed, the differences between the men themselves, this gift of near-naked men on display in my own living room, a room of my childhood.

I almost got started myself at an earlier age. Two high-school friends had joined a brand-new slick fitness center that had opened up in our neighborhood. Athletic teenagers, they made quick gains.

"It's great," said Mini (short for Minichiello), a muscly runt of an Italian. "Give it a try."

An enthusiastic fitness instructor expostulated on the benefits of free weights over machines, and a slightly disinterested promotions manager (but also fit, tall, and strong) tried to convince me of the benefits of membership.

"We'd fill in these parts here." He pointed to and lightly touched the indentations above my collarbone. My heart pounded wildly. When could I join?

Having no income at fifteen except a weekly allowance, I had to ask my parents. Would they help me? I had no idea, since I generally asked little from them.

"Would you really use it?" asked my father, who was not an athletic man. "I can't see you going."

"And what about school?" added my mother. "You've got a few months, and then summer, and then a new year. The membership is for a whole year. Do you know you'll use it that long?"

At the time, the answer was no. I didn't know, so I didn't argue. But in hindsight, of course I would have gone. And I probably would have even used the weights.

My attraction to muscle continued but became more realistic. When I finally did start going to the gym while in university, I learned how long it took to build up those comic-book muscles. I could tell which men worked out and which didn't, and I found out that the vast majority of regular fitness buffs didn't look anything like the men of my fantasies. Through my twenties, I cultivated a lust for more regularly athletic bodies and, in public, tried to tuck away my hot, panting tongue for the over-blown and over-defined.

This situation was compounded when I arrived in Sydney in 1999. My neck, used to gently turning from occasional glances at cute muscleboys, became strained from overuse and sudden craning. The flirtatious gay physiotherapist said it was a repetitive injury exacerbated possibly by a sharp, quick movement. "What sports are you doing?"

"Maybe something during my weight-training," I lied.

But Sweet Mother of God. How could I not look at the sudden blooming of my fantasies before my very eyes? Sydney was a town of gym queens and "Muscle Marys," a phrase I'd first heard in London. Did the strongest people from all over the country migrate to this one spot and breed? Was it because of the beach culture? A local shortage of fabric? Plain, dumb (but pretty) luck? Or some regulation about gay men having to work out? The gay men here were bodacious, bionic, and Barbie-onic.

Not only that, but during the famous dance parties—Sleaze, Mardi Gras, and more—musclemen from around the world would descend on this one place from London, Singapore, New York, Boston, Montreal, and L.A.

Could I have sex with one of them? Could I fulfill my fantasy?

The problem was that while I went to the gym and played sports, I could never muster up all the hours needed to become a Muscle Mary. And most Muscle Marys seemed to be attracted only to each other. It was the homo part of the word "homosexual" taken to a new level.

The other question I couldn't shake off was whether it wouldn't matter if I worked out every minute of the day. Would my ever-growing perfect body be passed over because it was an Asian and not a white one? I'd seen it happen before and knew it wasn't my imagination. Those of us on the bottom rungs of the ladder know who is on top, while those higher up are probably just staring at the view.

Still, I don't think about these things at all when I'm off my face, and once, on some miscellaneous dance party substance at a miscellaneous dance party, I wandered right into a towering 6' 5" mass of muscle—handsome too—though it was hard to notice his face with so many contours before me: biceps, chest, abdominals.

"Sorry," I said, and then I saw what I'd bumped into. "Can I have a hug?" My request clear above the music.

"Sure ..." he replied in an accent I identified as American South. He enveloped me in that flesh, and I was momentarily in the most amazing gay womb I could imagine.

Morgan rings me into his apartment, his voice scratchy through the security system. "Second floor, on the left, number sixteen."

He opens the door. I am nervous, wondering what would do me more good in this situation, more muscle or more confidence. The entranceway opened directly to the whole split-level apartment, an open kitchen which led down a flight of stairs to the bedroom below. I stand uncomfortably in his kitchen while we edge around each other with boxer's steps until he finally leans against the counter.

Business has been good, he tells me, and I can see that. He owns the apartment, and property is expensive in Sydney. I wonder how many windows he had to clean to buy it. And if it is this constant, physical work that keeps him so strong.

"What do you do?" he asks, without interest in the answer. Then, "So, are we going to do anything?"

I take this as an invitation, but still approach him as if he is either going to bite me or run away. I place my left hand on a shoulder as hard—even harder—than I expect and lean over to kiss him. He turns his head and I end up nuzzling his neck and ear.

"C'mon, mate." He leads me down the stairs, to the bedroom.

I push him onto the bed and lay on top of him, still aiming for a kiss. He writhes below me, and his body is like nothing I've felt before, as if it isn't one piece but many pieces moving and shifting in relation to each other.

"This is different," he says.

Different from what? I think.

He lets me into his mouth but I'm not paying attention, frankly. My hands are roaming his body, exploring. He has those big winged muscles under his arms that curve from the back to the top of the stomach. His pectorals through his shirt are perfectly parted with a ridged indentation in between them, like the spine of a small animal. I slip my hand beneath his T-shirt and up onto his back. It is volcanic, like molten ash hardened into ridges and contours, still warm.

I throw off my shirt, hurriedly, awkwardly.

"You're bigger than I thought you were," he comments.

Wait until you see my cock, I think, but furrow my brow. He sounds surprised instead of excited. I grab his T-shirt and pull upwards. He collaborates and lifts his arms up, and the shirt comes off in one motion. I gasp. His body is as I remembered it, round muscles defined with sharp lines. But maybe even more beautiful. I bury my head in those muscles like a pig in slop, like I am in some human food contest, my hands tied behind my back and my mouth down in the Jell-O, spaghetti, giant chocolate sundaes. The soft edible bits have all been consumed and my tongue now scrapes the bottom of the bowl, hard rounded glass.

His nipples are especially delicious, neither tiny nor large. Still, they stick out, rubbery offerings with just enough give in them to suck and nibble while he continues squirming below me like a snake shedding skin. His blue jeans come off, then my army shorts. His hand goes to my underwear, the outline of my cock. He pulls at the waistband with his index finger and looks inside.

"You're big. I haven't seen an Asian with a cock like this."

I would take it as misguided flattery, but it isn't. His comment has authority but wants no favor. He grabs the long shaft of my penis and starts pumping rhythmically. I reach over to reciprocate, and feel the texture of his balls, relaxed and giving. They spill out of my palm perfectly. His cock is a small, fat sausage—warm, but not erect. I step off the bed, grab his jock by the waistband, and haul it off, lifting his legs into a pair of scissors.

"This is different," he says again.

I dive down onto his groin and envelope his cock with my mouth.

I roll it around with my tongue and feel blood filling the chambers. I reach my arms up to run down his torso, which to me is the most amazing part of Morgan's body. His stomach is like the underside of a tortoise shell: each section a plate of armor welded into place, side by side, into perfect arrangement. It actually stands out from the rest of his body. His chest muscles are big and round enough to jut out past his abdomen. But unlike other men I'd seen, whose midsections dipped slightly concave like a cracked bowl, or most men, whose stomachs flattened if lucky, but mostly softened, Morgan's is hard and convex. Just putting my hand on it sends electric pulses racing between my shoulders and groin and ricocheting in-between.

My hand reaches around to his arse. I don't even think about it. It just slides around his hard buttocks and through his legs. I pause from sucking to spit on my finger and then match the rhythm of my blowjob with my finger sliding into his anus simultaneously. It slips into a tight spot easily like a London driver squeezing into parking in the center of the city. Morgan groans, the loudest sound that I've heard him make so far. I continue for a few seconds then work my way up with my mouth through the maze of crevices and pathways, knowing I won't get lost.

Again, face to face. His features look old in this light and his lips are chapped. Did he lick them all day long? He is still only semi-erect.

"Sorry. I'm a little nervous tonight."

I'm too filled with lust to worry why he's nervous or wonder if he's not attracted to me. I'm horny, selfish, and unable to breathe calmly. I shift behind him. I want to feel what it would be like to hold him from behind. I bite his neck and squeeze his chest hard.

"This is different."

Then, I can't help myself. My tongue is dragged through the labyrinth again to end up at the exit or entrance, a round hole, a radius, arrows pointing in or out. My tongue fits perfectly where my finger was earlier.

It's hard to decide whether to place my hands on his back, sides, or legs—they're all rippling in different but intriguing ways. Do I just part his buttocks like the Red Sea and walk and walk and walk? Continuing with the theme of gluttony, I decide to do a bit of each.

"There's rubbers over there," he points.

Did I hear right? It's like an invitation to go to a restaurant I didn't think I could afford. True, he's not going to fuck me with a half-limp dick, and I'm glad for that since I'm an awkward bottom. But this is unexpected. Unexpectedly good.

I reach over. There are condoms and sachets of lube in a drawer. I grab one, rip it open, and take a few lube packets in the other hand. I wish he had a bottle rather than these free, fiddly things. He's still on his stomach, just lying there, kind of looking back to watch me.

"I might be a little tight."

But I've got the rubber on and have slathered two sachets of jelly up and down my shaft and the remainder on his asshole. My cock slides in in two stages, just a short pause after the first, and then it's all the way in, and he's writhing and twisting beneath me.

I put my hands on his stomach from behind him and it feels like I'm gripping the bar of a roller coaster, my stomach lurching with excitement and exhilaration. I'm sitting (kneeling actually) bolt up-right, but the world is whooshing past me, sending things in and out of focus.

The image I'm looking for suddenly strikes me. He's some sort of arthropod, part of the ninety percent of the animal kingdom that wears its skeleton on the outside of its body, like the plates of a prawn or lobster. I know, not very erotic until you tear it open and suck the sweet flesh right out. But the hard moving parts are like no human I've touched, and somehow I like it. How will I ever re-create this?

I'm mostly just riding him, my cock as far inside of him as it will go, when I feel a spasm, that little signal that my excitement is boiling over.

No, I don't want it to happen. I've been fucking him for no

longer than two minutes. Shit! I'm too excited, this is too exciting, I—Ai—Ay. Ohh.

My body shudders, I can't pretend anything else is happening. I'm coming. The last bit of jizz shoots out of me and into the condom and there's a sudden drop of temperature as if the sun has ducked behind a cloud.

"That was quick."

"Sorry. Uh, do you want to come?"

"No, mate." His body is covered in a thin coat of sweat. He looks down at his dick. "I don't know what's wrong with it tonight."

I consider kissing him again but think better of it. He's not much for kissing.

"When I saw you in the gym, I didn't think you were so big."

"Really?"

"I usually go for guys thinner than you. Not so muscular."

I picture myself as a woolly mammoth. "Is that your boyfriend?" I've spotted a photo of two people on his dresser.

"Yeah, I have a boyfriend."

Things are becoming clearer.

"He lives with his parents out in Parramatta. He comes in two nights a week—on Thursdays and then on Saturdays."

"Can I have a shower?"

I shower with Morgan. I soap his body down front and back, my hands up and down his legs. It's quick; he submits but does not let himself go.

So, that was what was different. A muscular Asian boy, aggressive, with a long cock. Who fucked him. Not a young, slight, passive Asian boy who lives with his parents. That was different.

I know I shouldn't push it. I want more, and I know that to get more, the key is to play it cool. He's invited me to call him again, and I will.

I'm away on a work trip for two weeks. This gives me ample time to pretend I'm more casual about it than I am. (Casual is not jacking off every night fantasizing about fucking him again.) I dream of no early ejaculation for me and a hard dick for him. A proper fuck-session, if I can control myself. If I can't, maybe he'll let me practice.

I can tell he's not a phone person when I call him. The conversation is curt and to the point, and I can't ascertain from the tone of his voice whether he's happy to hear from me.

"Monday," he says, disappointing me, since it's Wednesday. "I'll be free on Monday night. Call after work."

I figure it's not a good idea to look a gift horse in the mouth. Maybe someone horse-hung, but in that situation it would be my mouth I'd be concentrating on, not his.

I spend five days and five nights in a pent-up state. I'm horny and I want sex, but I've decided who I want sex with. I wonder whether to call another man I had sex with last month, but it's only Morgan who's going to scratch this itch. As well, I'm finding it hard settling into the new city. No boyfriends in sight. Not enough friends. Work is stressing me out. I want a fuck. I want Morgan. I want to lose myself in his muscles.

On Monday, I wait all day and then some more. I radiate anticipation, so much so that my flatmate walks by and asks me if I'm arranging some trade.

"Hope so," I reply and dial the number.

It rings. And rings. After the seventh tone, the answering machine clicks in. It's his same gruff voice and a nondescript message.

"Hey, Morgan. Give me a call when you get in." I leave my phone number. Then I pace around, decide to make dinner, make dinner, and wolf it down as quickly as possible in case he calls so I have time digest it before seeing him.

I call again. This is the message I leave: "Hey, Morgan. I thought we were supposed to get together tonight. Give me a call." I'm edgy now. I'm bad when something I've planned to do in the evening falls apart; I psyche myself up to do it and find it hard to redirect my energy. And I hate that I don't yet have friends who I can call any time and say, hey, I'm bored, let's go out for a drink.

It's worse that I've been stood up a few times lately by acquaintances. This new-guy-in-town thing; it's up to me to find their rhythms, fit into their schedules, make the proposal and double-check the date. I don't always double-check, which leaves me with evenings yawning and stretching their way out before me, taunting me to fill them with something other than jacking off and going to sleep early.

Where is he? Fuck.

I go out for a walk. I have nothing to do. I consider dropping by his place but can't remember the apartment number, and even if I did, I know it would be the wrong thing to do. When I return to my apartment it's late, but not too late to fuck, and still too early to sleep. I leave one last message:

"Sorry we couldn't catch up tonight. I'll call again sometime to find out when you're free."

Two days later I'm still burning with lust and frustration, so I call. "Hi, Morgan, it's …" He hangs up. Wait—did that just happen? I call again and the line is busy.

It's two weeks later when I run into him on the street. He pauses, and I can feel his anger. He doesn't know whether to walk right by or not.

"Look, Morgan. Whatever it is, I'm sorry, can you tell me …" I've picked up this righteous tone in my voice.

"He was there."

I shut up. I swallow.

"He heard the messages."

It sinks in what happened.

"I had to tell him."

It sinks in. "I …" I fix him with a stare, and no longer see the bodybuilder of my dreams. I see an upset older man with a terrific body who is not much of a talker and wants to get away from me as soon as possible.

"I'm sorry, Morgan. It was stupid of me to do that. I won't call again."

He grumbles something that I take as consent, and I watch him walk away, his footsteps resigned and sad. I feel my long rubber-sheathed cock up his muscular arse, my hands at the top of his armor of stomach muscles, and the calamity of movement below me as his musculature shifts back and forth between the four directions. I make a note to myself to try to hang onto this physical memory for as long as I can because I know it's the last I'll ever feel of it.

Army of Ugly

Daniel Allen Cox

It was 1995, when the Internet took too long, and when we were all beautiful over the phone.

We met on a chat line. I tweaked on how he kept calling me "squirt," and we hooked up on his birthday at a downtown strip club littered with pastel balloons. I ditched him almost as soon as I got there because he didn't fit my shallow beauty standards. I guess I expected him to be someone else.

The next day, he called me from a payphone to say that he'd gotten bashed after leaving the club alone, and that he was now deaf in one ear.

Today, thirteen years later, I want to whisper into his good ear that I shouldn't have left. Not because he was bashed, which I might not have been able to prevent, but because we are all ugly. I want to whisper that we need to start a revolution. I might hug him, too.

When I say "ugly," I mean, "beautifully uncloned."

Physical differentiators, I've just begun to realize, have always driven me wild. I have been known to fawn over a prominent nose or larynx, to worship an extra nipple, and to lustily trace the line of a slightly crooked fang. Ear quirks are yummy, too. These personal trademarks are what make us attractive, and intolerance of them is what makes us ugly.

It was 1979, when I was three, and when Montreal still had a baseball team. I fell off a bleacher seat at the Olympic Stadium, kissed the concrete, and gave myself a bloody second eyebrow. The childhood scar grew with me, but nobody ever talks about it. Why not? In Bruce LaBruce's film, *Otto; or, Up with Dead People*, the gay zombies with their pretty facial gashes may turn some people off, but it means unquenchable necromancy for the rest of us.

Those abdominal fuck-holes that Bruce has given his undead *beau laide:* I want one.

People will sometimes find me reading a book, hand clutching the threadbare crotch of my pants. It's true. They'll find me spending time with literature's ugliest and most erotic creatures. Who hasn't masturbated to Evie Cottrell from Chuck Palahniuk's *Invisible Monsters*, a homicidal nymph with heat-scorched hair, wearing an incinerated wedding dress, cocking a rifle at the top of a staircase in a raging house fire?

I am equally in thrall to the bar creep in *Giovanni's Room*, the only book I have ever read twice. Author James Baldwin describes him as "a mummy or zombie," whose "thin, black hair was violent with oil." Here's some more foreplay: "… the face was white and thoroughly bloodless … the shirt, open coquettishly to the navel, revealed a hairless chest and a silver crucifix … He had been eating garlic and his teeth were very bad."

Too many freckles, I want, and a grenade-shaped birthmark. A spotted dick like a post-Oreo blowjob I can't wash off.

It was 2002, when the undead still walked the streets. I ran into the half-deaf guy downtown. We locked eyes, I tried to transform recognition into a vacant stare, and, like a shithead, I kept on walking.

Perhaps you celebrate physical diversity and have much to teach us. If more people voice their preference for the unconventional, teens might spend less time lavishing hate on their changing bodies, and their skin might become a more comfortable home for them. Escort agencies will hire people who look different, porn companies will shoot them, and strip clubs will include them in the nightly rotation. The unique will use their differentiators to get ahead in the sex industry, in the arts, and in life. You'll suddenly have greater access to the people who turn you on, because you said something.

Think about this: Every time you post a Craigslist personals ad that ends with "looks not important," you bring everybody one stroke closer to orgasm.

It was 2008, when buffet restaurants were still the shit. Bruce LaBruce had just introduced me to Cointreau, after teaching the equally clueless waiter the meaning of "on the rocks." We hopped a cab with a mickey of rum and drank our way to the nearest strip club to continue my education in the finer points of life.

The place looked familiar, what with the deflated balloons in Key lime and baby blue.

Bruce was roundly unimpressed with the dancers, until one strutted onstage that had him breaking his teeth on a stir stick. "What's so special about this guy? Steroids have turned him into a giant varicose vein," I said.

"That's why," Bruce answered. "He's ugly." His words gave me a blood surge. The revolution felt closer than ever.

Fangs I want more than anything else. The revolution would call for a good set of teeth.

It's 2009, and I've reached the breaking point. I turn to the only place where zombies like me can shed their remaining prejudices: the Internet. Here, in its entirety, is the Craigslist ad that I posted under "missed connections," my message in a bottle of ether:

"It was 1995. I ditched you on your birthday, and I've sucked bat shit ever since. Now I find you hotter than Evie Cottrell (will explain). Please answer back so you can clock me in the mouth, or so we can fuck on the Olympic Stadium concrete (will explain that, too). P.S. Deaf boys are sexy."

We can all be beautiful over the Internet, right?

AMANUENSIS
Steve MacIsaac

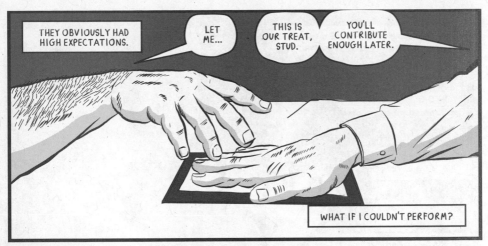

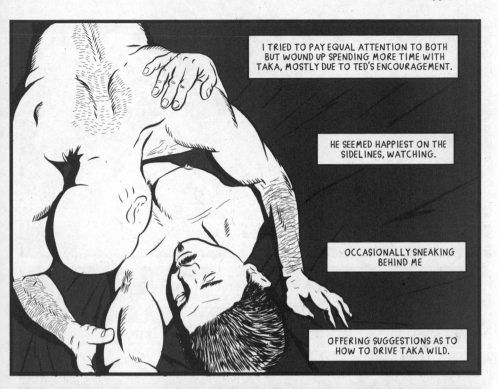

I TRIED TO PAY EQUAL ATTENTION TO BOTH BUT WOUND UP SPENDING MORE TIME WITH TAKA, MOSTLY DUE TO TED'S ENCOURAGEMENT.

HE SEEMED HAPPIEST ON THE SIDELINES, WATCHING.

OCCASIONALLY SNEAKING BEHIND ME

OFFERING SUGGESTIONS AS TO HOW TO DRIVE TAKA WILD.

WHEN TAKA WAS ABOUT TO COME TED LAY DOWN NEXT TO HIM, WHISPERING INTO HIS EAR.

THE MORE PLEASURE TAKA FELT, THE MORE INTENSELY THEY WOULD TOUCH AND FONDLE EACH OTHER.

THEY WERE KISSING MADLY WHEN TAKA CAME.

EYES ONLY FOR EACH OTHER

LIKE I WASN'T EVEN IN THE ROOM.

The Day the Men Came for Good

Landon Dixon

I started having rape fantasies in high school. Solid, smooth-bodied men taking me by force, pinning me on the bed-liner in the back of a raunchy van or on a soft, pine-needled forest bed warmed by the summer sun, and kissing me, thrusting their hard tongues into my mouth, bending their rugged heads down to suck insistently on my scared-stiff nipples, their strong hands holding my arms down, their muscled bodies grinding into my more slender self. I whimpered and writhed, but I couldn't—wouldn't—get loose.

These hard-bodied men never did anything more than smother me with their mouths and bodies. They never raped me, because I wasn't sure of the how and the where of what came after being pinned, kissed, and tongued. While my friends were dreaming about seducing our exotic French teacher, or the snobbish new big-breasted blonde whose dad had just bought the local farm implements dealership, those uncompromising, hunky men were forcing their way into my dreamy fantasies and my awakening consciousness. Making me submit to what I could not—would not—acknowledge.

Strict upbringing in a conservative household in small-town Manitoba forced me to sublimate my true nature, made me want the men to take me by force, rather than through mutual attraction. Although I didn't know that at the time.

I dated girls, even made out with girls, the class slut and I getting as far as heavy petting before an RCMP officer rousted us behind the grain elevator. But it was passive and uninspired on my part. Emotional heat didn't flare up to southwestern-Manitoba-in-summer levels—except at night in the tiny, stuffy third-floor confines of my bedroom, or in stifling, steam-heated winter classrooms. That's when the men of my unformed fantasies took me panting and squirming, forcing me to focus, however confusedly, on what really turned me on.

So when I escaped to university in big-city Winnipeg and was on my own for the first time in my life (my parents and brothers and sisters and all of my graduating class were 200 miles southwest), I was ready to explore what I was all about sexually. I started to notice real guys, for the first time openly admiring their bodies and faces, the way they walked and ran, talked and laughed and smelled. The way their eyes twinkled and their cheeks dimpled and their thick, pink tongues moistened their full, red lips, teeth gleaming white. The way they filled out a T-shirt, nipples clearly and eagerly visible to the discerning eye. The way they filled out a pair of acid-washed jeans, their tight, bitable buttocks straining faded, riveted fabric.

And though I was enrolled in engineering, I started writing, putting my fantasies down on paper.

Still too timid to even consider opening up to another guy—fear of irrevocably revealing myself and fear of brutal rejection mixing in equal toxic, irrational quantities—I took the next logical step: documenting my feelings and fantasies. The men coming from my fevered imagination and filling pages forced me to confront my bent orientation, their kisses heavier and wetter and more real in ink, their bodies hotter and harder on the written page, their imagined bared cocks grinding into and inflaming my willing and ready cock.

This early writing consisted of one-act sex pieces transcribed word-for-word and act-for-act from my sexual fantasies. Tough, handsome, sweat-slicked, and smooth-skinned studs stepped out of the glossy pages of *Sports Illustrated* and *National Geographic* and the Technicolor ether of *Top Gun* and *Conan the Barbarian*, growling with grunts and groans the obligatory (at least to my mind), "You know you like it!" as the men of my desires manhandled me, smothering my increasingly feeble protestations with their knowing lips and tongues and hands, enveloping my trembling, virginal body with their rugged, masculine physiques.

William Shakespeare or John Preston I wasn't. The stories often climaxed prematurely, The End coming well before plot and character were fully developed, as I humped my dormitory bed and closed my eyes and dropped my pen, or slid a hand below the library study carrel desktop and grabbed and squeezed and rubbed. Every story had the same messy ending, with nothing resolved, least of all my nerve.

Until one day when, sprawled on my dorm room bed penning another wet dream fantasy when I should've been writing a term paper for Fluid Mechanics, a real live man appeared, bringing me that much closer to my ultimate sexual destiny.

The yarn I was writing that day involved the aloof, arrogant Dynamics and Vibrations class teaching assistant. In my imagination, he had me pinned, naked, up against the fourth floor engineering building classroom blackboard, forcing his full, wet lips against my trembling mouth, his lean body mashing mine. The classroom was as empty as the dormitory that dreary end-of-spring-break Friday afternoon. Rafael and I were naked, and he was muscling my arms over my head, licking and biting my neck. His hard cock jousted with my straining prick. As I scribbled my story, the resultant tingle was weird and wonderful.

As I pumped my hips, the wooden dorm bed creaked while words poured out of my quivering mechanical pencil tip onto lined graph paper, a crude climax promising to cap, as usual, my less-than-literary composition.

"Workin' on an assignment, Poindexter?"

I froze like the prairies in January.

"Old man Frohlinger's class, huh?"

It was Lyle, the guy two doors down from my room. He was in my Fluid Mechanics class, a loud redhead on the football reserve squad, always chugging everyone under the table at the Red Lion Friday-night beer bashes. Good looking in a rawboned, Biff

Tannen from *Back to the Future* way. Smart and smart-assed.

He strode over and ripped the spiral notebook from my hands. "These don't look like the notes *I* took in class." He laughed, scanning my almost incomprehensible handwriting.

I sprang off the bed and grabbed at the notebook, desperate to retrieve the explicit confession, my hard-on gone to soft-on, my emotions from excitement to shame. The engineering faculty had a well-earned reputation as the least broad-minded of all campus disciplines; Engineering-Week strippers and smut movie antics were still at full ribald tilt back then.

Lyle easily held the offending notebook up and out of my reach with a long arm, his other hand on my chest, restraining me while he kept reading. I frantically grabbed his broad shoulders and hooked a foot around one of his ankles, trying to push him off balance so that he'd drop the incriminating scribbling.

But he was too strong, too quick on his feet. In a flash he had me pinned flat on my back on the bed, his left arm across my chest, right hand still gripping my notebook, reading and laughing.

"Sorta like this, huh, pervert?" he said, pumping his hips, pressing his crotch into my crotch, his football-buffed body stretched over mine.

And in that volatile instant, I came out. I stopped struggling. A warm wave of undeniable pleasure, centered on Lyle's jeaned cock grinding into my jeaned cock, washed through me. I reveled in the physical contact.

"You're one sick little fuck," Lyle laughed, his breath in my face hot and humid and bubblegum flavored. "Gettin' off on jumping a broad and having your way with her, huh?"

That's how he read it, anyway. We were so naïve back then, before the days of Internet porn and gay cowboy movies. My bad handwriting helped, too.

"Better build up a little muscle, loverboy, if you wanna be the one on top," Lyle advised, grinning down at me. He pumped his cock onto mine, his powerful loins flooding me with lust, his musky scent making my head spin.

He dropped the notebook and grabbed my shoulders, thrusting harder and faster, his freckled face inches from mine, his white teeth clenched, sweat sheening his broad forehead. "This is how you do it, in case you didn't know!" he rasped, getting into the role of playing friendly neighborhood rapist—little realizing that only one of us was playing. He torqued up the pressure, pumping me so hard the bed rattled against the concrete wall. "You like it, huh?"

I whimpered, playing along, feeding into and off of Lyle's aggressive strength, anxious to keep the erotic game going as long as possible. I spread my legs so that his rigid cock slid along the length of mine.

I stared into his glittering blue eyes and moaned, squirming, then wrenched my arms out of his grasp and boldly grabbed his mounded butt cheeks.

"Fuckin' slut!" he growled, pumping harder, faster. My fingernails dug into his flexing buttocks, spurring him on.

Then, suddenly, shockingly, as he dry-fucked me, Lyle kissed my peach-fuzzed cheeks with fierce, dry kisses. Recklessly, I covered Lyle's lush lips with my own, kissing back.

"Easy, tiger," Lyle said, rolling off me and jumping to his feet. He laughed nervously, sweeping a pale hand through his thick red hair and looking at me, laid out on the bed, a happy smile on my face. "People'll think you're queer. Let me know when you really get goin' on that assignment—and we'll compare notes."

Then he was gone, leaving me fuzzy with wonder, and contentment.

Unfortunately, the promise of Lyle's parting words was not to be fulfilled, as it would have been in a well-written erotic story: Lyle was as heterosexual as Hugh Hefner on testosterone. Our sex play meant nothing to him.

But it had meant the world to me. It was the soul-satisfying conflagration point where wishful juvenile fantasy and revealing adult reality collided with an explosive climax, confirming my sexual identity and launching me on a lifetime of true gay experiences—and on a career writing queer porn.

It was the day the men came for good.

Dawn of the Dad

Shawn Syms

I look you in the eye. You glance at your feet. Neither of us moves until your gaze meets mine again. My arms stretch out. Your head tilts downward as you move toward me, the thin hair of your light beard meshing with the thick black curls on my chest. I imagine that your eyes are closed, and place my hand at the back of your neck with calm authority. I don't need to tell you what to do.

You lower yourself, spend an appropriate amount of time down on your knees, mouth full and jaw challenged. Then, when I choose, you're bent over in front of me on the bed. I grab an ass cheek, place a hand on your shoulder blade, position you with a firm grip on each nipple, pull on one of your ears, slap lightly at your face. You hint at seeking escape and inch away from my mauling. But the bed is up against a wall, and before you know it, you're backed into a corner. I smack your nuts once with my knuckles; you wince and freeze.

"Hold still, Son," I say, easing on a rubber and applying lube. Entering you, I pretend to ignore any sound you make. Once I'm fully inside, I stay completely still until you say it.

"Fuck me, Dad." Your head lowered, barely a whisper.

I begin and don't stop until your Daddy's hefty load is drilled deep into your consciousness. I put you in a headlock when I start to cum. You cry as I unload. I take it for granted that these are tears of joy. After all, father knows best, right?

Who's your Daddy? The archetype of the father/son relationship is one paradigm that can be used to understand and experience queer men's consensual sexuality and relationships. The idea may not work for everyone, but it's long been a potent conceptual framework for me.

Whether it contains overt role-playing or not, sometimes the way two adult men relate to one another—in bed and out—can have aspects of the familial and paternal, with someone who seems "older and wiser" taking charge and offering encouragement and support to someone else who needs it.

Like most sexuality, a lot of father/son lust takes place as much in one's psyche as in the real world, a hormonally driven re-factoring of internalized messages about the relationship between fathers and sons. Whether your ideal vision of Dad is someone stern who must be obeyed or a loving conveyor of life lessons, these images can slumber stubbornly in your gonads into adulthood, when they awake to greedily seek an appropriate outlet.

Any sort of sexual roleplay illuminates the powerful lure of the imaginary in our lives. While exploring a situation that's barely conceivable in a consensual context—having sex with your own father—it's possible to create vivid erotic tableaux that blend the emotional with the corporeal, combining remembrances of one's own upbringing with contemplations of the meaning of reproduction itself. And some pretty intense orgasms.

What does "Dad sex" look like? There are probably as many answers as there are men with filial leanings or paternal urges. For me, probably the most highly charged and fulfilling thing I can do with another man is to put my arm around him and place his head gently on my chest. It makes me feel loving and protective in a fatherly way.

The urge to relate to another man in a paternally affectionate way comes up a lot in my sexual friendships. From my perspective this has to do with an overarching impulse to support, protect, nurture, and encourage others. That can become eroticized, but has a genuine emotional aspect too. It even plays out in rewarding ways during encounters with men I meet in passing. To hold someone in your arms and let him lose himself there—even if it's someone you may never see again—feels like an expression of love, a way of seeing him off into the world with care and respect, the way a father might with a departing son.

But cuddling aside, I also get a lot of satisfaction from the rougher side of Dad/son action. All rhetoric about the righteousness of versatility goes out the window—a submissive son will consider my orgasm his reward. And finding a guy who needs a take-charge Daddy is not hard. Many men have an urge to capitulate, or a desire to be taken care of—they appreciate a firm hand, someone who is eager to be aggressive with them. I've learned it's pretty straightforward to get another guy to submit to your will—and that's a responsibility I take seriously.

I am reminded of a story about a guy who was turned on by pissing into other men's mouths. He didn't want to have any discussion about it, or issue a safe word to be gargled in the event of urine overflow. He didn't even give any warnings. When he got a sense that the guy with a mouthful of cock might be into it, he just started to piss, to see what would happen. For Dads seeking sons, it's pretty much the same. Sometimes, when you fuck a certain way, a man will automatically call you Daddy. Sometimes it's a look you give him, a firm hand on his shoulder, or the way you start to become instructive. Other times, you just use the word son, and see what follows.

To me, being a Dad is about mindset rather than chronological age differences. In the encounter I described at the outset of this essay, I called a man only a year younger than me my son. The first time a guy called me Daddy in a sexual context, I was in my early twenties. And I often find myself attracted to mature men who are old enough to be someone's biological father—or even grandfather—but once we're alone the expected roles are reversed. To play on a sexual expression from the 1970s, they are Dads on the streets and sons in the sheets!

In some fetishized communities—such as the realms of bears—

there is a lot misplaced agonizing over the question of who counts as a bear, what makes a cub, how many white hairs you need to be called a polar bear, etc. When it comes to Dads and sons, much could be made of a requirement for an age difference or enactment of domination and submission.

As far as I'm concerned, the question of who is a Dad is pretty simple—whoever can pull it off to the satisfaction of a willing son. Sexual exploration is all about expanding the boundaries of what can be imagined, making it a source of some of life's richest and most unexpected possibilities. One man I call son was born female. Sometimes when we play he inhabits what he experiences as the emotional and psychological mind-space of a five-year-old male child. What he's thinking about may be different from what I'm imagining at the same time, but the encounter still works for both of us.

The father/son sexual dynamic has found a place in gay men's erotic representations over time, complicating the meanings of family, heterosexuality, and masculinity in the process. Historic pulp fiction like Karl Flinders' *Up Daddy* can today be found in a special collection at New York University. In that novel, straight protagonist Brewster Steele teaches his two teen sons to screw his butt, ostensibly as a fix for persistent prostate problems. And Joe Gage's seminal 1970s porn film, *El Paso Wrecking Corp.*, features a father and son in the same sex scene.

But what does it mean in real life for two adult men to fulfill these roles? Is using the words father and son during intimate encounters an insult to those who have faced actual sexual abuse in incestuous circumstances? In the same way that S/M sexuality is not equivalent to unprovoked violence, consensual Dad sex isn't the same as child sex abuse.

I do have an acquaintance who sucked off his uncle multiple times while both of them were well above the age of consent—but I suspect his experience is uncommon. On the other hand, one boy-identified friend of mine thinks something may have happened to him when he was a child—leaving me to wonder if aspects of his sex life may comprise a form of therapy. A few guys I know who are almost exclusively attracted to older father figures have poor or non-existent relationships with their real-life male parents. Meanwhile, my own bond with my biological father gets stronger with each passing year.

As I near the age of forty, I'm not sure if actual fatherhood is in the cards for me. But, if anything, fitting comfortably in an erotic Daddy role feels to me like a special sort of self-actualization, a coming-to-terms with my own masculinity and experience of aging. As a child, I fit the stereotype of the queer kid who was acutely aware of being different, and was ostracized from others as a result. My sense of what made a man was colored by my impressions of the fathers in my working-class neighborhood, burly guys who worked at General Motors and seemed comfortable in their own skins. Growing up, I felt alien, and never imagined that I could be anything like those men. Today, I feel differently. Like a lot of transmen I know, I've learned that masculine identity is something you can have an active hand in creating.

What does any of this say about my relationship with my own father? As a very little boy I was closer to my mother and felt I had the most in common with her. Maybe it was harder to get to know my father back then; at the time he struck me above all as a big, loud man who slept at weird times (he was a shift worker). While I share a very strong bond with my amazing mom, the older I get the more I realize how I take after my father. I'm now proud to try to emulate him.

My father truly represents what's often referred to as a self-made man. He was fatherless and impoverished at five, orphaned at eleven. The youngest child in his family, he was hauled across the Atlantic Ocean to a new country and shuffled around from one indifferent older sibling to another. By thirteen he was on his own, sometimes sleeping in ditches. But before long he was working alongside grown men, paying his own bills, and raising his own family.

We moved a lot when I was a kid. That was a social challenge with lots of repercussions—but it was because my father was driven to always do better for his family. My father is kind, down-to-earth, hilariously funny, practical, worldly wise, and caring; someone who has strived to improve the lives of those closest to him. Who wouldn't want to be more like that?

Perhaps my ultimate goal with all the men in my life—friends and lovers alike—is to earn their trust and respect, to give them reasons to look up to me the same way I admire my own dad.

Wednesdays at Six

Kevin Alderson

When and where did I place that ad? I had completely forgotten about it, until I spotted the "I am interested" subject line on an email. Interested in what? I wondered.

I anxiously opened the email to read, "I found your ad on ____, and are you interested in getting together? I am 23 years old and have a nice cock. Enjoy amateur erotic wrestling—nude and oil okay. I am 5' 11", 220 lb."

Fetish wrestling? Kind of like having a memory from childhood and not knowing for sure whether it really happened or if you just dreamt it. For reasons I didn't understand then, however, I knew I was looking for a plethora of different sexual experiences, and kink was definitely "it" that day.

But my God, I thought, he outweighs me by fifty pounds. He didn't describe himself as muscular, but what if he was? I'd be destroyed in minutes! My desire grew in intensity, however, so after a few emails, we agreed to get together—Wednesday at six p.m.

When I tell my live-in boyfriend about what I have arranged, he responds with his typical "Okay." I've bought a large blue polyethylene tarp to cover the furniture and carpet in the basement of our 1918 house. With two blue lights situated strategically over the wrestling area, I have created a dark, sultry atmosphere, oozing an aura of dirty sex.

Now it is nearly six p.m. and anxiety surfaces. Do I have everything—olive oil, pot, booze, condoms, lube, trance music? I'm already turned on, wearing faded blue jeans, shirtless with bare feet, my usual home attire.

The doorbell pierces through the music. Not knowing what to expect, I am initially surprised to see a pudgy young man with glasses standing in front of me. He looks similarly shocked as he stares at my perky pecs.

"Hi. I'm Don."

"I'm Kevin. Come in." Jolted by the reality that I was about to wrestle, I wonder what he thinks of me. He soon lets me know:

"You're hot. I didn't know what to expect when you told me you're thirty-six." Thanks to the gym, I can still pass for thirty-six, a lie of about ten years.

"I know what you mean," I say, pretending nonchalance. "Would you like to smoke up first?"

"For sure."

I light the joint, pour rye and diet Coke, and offer both. We sit, talk, smoke, drink, and learn a little about each other. After the joint, we are baked, and I say, "Want to start?"

"Sounds good."

Yikes, I'm thinking. What the hell have I got myself into? I feel my age as I traipse down the stairs.

Once in the basement, I kiss his lips. He reciprocates fully while kneading my firm pecs and tweaking my nipples. I'm excited. I pull off his shirt and twist his nipples hard—testing to see what this sissy boy can take. He unzips my jeans and grabs my pouch, squeezing my engorged cock. My body quivers with excitement and apprehension. I peel off his jeans and grab his nuts with a "know-who's-boss" attitude, smirking as I stare into his eyes. He succumbs at first, then musters a similar smirk. "You're gonna pay for that, bitch!" I like his attitude.

We spread oil liberally over our bodies. His extra heft could be a problem, but I am too excited to stop. We grapple, but the oil at first foils our attempts at a hold, so we exchange light punches, avoiding only the head and face.

But ball shots are okay, so every now and then pain surges into my gut, an old familiar feeling from the wonder years. We have set few rules, and winner takes all, so unless one of us really wants to be bottomed out, there is strong incentive to win. "Winning" comes when either Don or I are simply too tired to continue wrestling, or through submission.

Over the weeks that followed, his weight and youth were nicely balanced by my greater muscularity: who won was always unpredictable. As weeks turned into months, winning and losing vaporized with every encounter. Bonds of friendship developed as sex and aggression blended. The merely physical transformed into a deeper connection that remains alive today, long after I injured my shoulder, thus ending both our wrestling adventures and one aspect of my midlife crisis.

Funny how caught up we get in the "isms," even when, as gay people, we should know better. I am not talking about heterosexism, racism, or sexism. I mean ageism—and whatever the -ism is that refers to our avoidance of getting into committed relationships with someone who struggles with weight. Don and I occasionally talked about being in a relationship. His issue was that I was twice his age—since our first encounter, I had let him know how old I really was. My issue was his size. Gay culture has not been kind to overweight men. Both images—middle-aged and fat—stand in stark contrast to the gay male ideal of a young, well-muscled Adonis. Our barriers, partly self-created, but mostly given to us by well-meaning others, prevented us from moving beyond hot wrestling and a good friendship.

As a reflective person who tries to figure out every part of what makes me tick, I often wondered why I desired my wrestling escapades. Being close with another man and feeling his body strain was exciting unto itself, but in hindsight, I believe the most important dynamic was that I wanted to recapture my fading youth, knowing at a deep level that aging was already taking a toll on my looks and my energy. And what I learned is that wrestling did indeed keep me young.

Feeling young is about living fully in every moment. Every time my muscles struggled to meet Don's strength, I felt fully alive, knowing that every punch and every bodily contortion was symbolic of a fight going on at a deeper, intra-psychic level. Beyond stamina, strength, and wrinkles, however, lay the determination to try new things.

While you are trying new things, you are too engrossed to think about your age. Thinking about Wednesdays at six still brings a smile to my face. The challenges I faced each Wednesday at six kept my spirit singing happily. Maybe six will also become your lucky number.

The Eroticism of Football: Thank You, Jim Harbaugh

Aaron Hamburger

It isn't always easy being a gay football fan.

First, there's the obvious discomfort of standing in a stadium of red-blooded heterosexual men screaming out speculations about the bedroom proclivities of their opponents. For example: last year, while on my way to Michigan Stadium to cheer on my beloved Wolverines, I noticed one of the hottest-selling T-shirts for sale had renamed Jim Tressel, coach of our hated archrival, Ohio State, "Brokeback Tressel." (In much of America, *Brokeback Mountain* has now become a synonym for "gay," which is often a synonym for "anyone I dislike.")

There's also the less obvious discomfort caused by revealing your predilections outside the football world. Since moving to New York, I have been a writer and teacher of writing for several years. When the subject of that most macho of sports has come up in conversation, many of my fellow writers, artists, friends, even potential dates have gawked at me in shock or horror, then asked, "You like football?"

No, I don't like football. I'm passionate about the sport. Each year as fall approaches, I buy any magazine I can find marked "football preview" on the cover. When the season begins, my boyfriend makes himself scarce as I park myself in front of the TV on college football Saturdays from noon to midnight. I love the gaudy uniforms and the tacky mascots. I love the blasts of referees' whistles, the vicious clicks of pads hitting pads, the throaty play calls, the rising roar from the crowd as a ball lofts high in the air. I love studying the hard stats of attempts and completions, yards per carry, sacks, turnovers. I love the wavelike rhythm of the game itself, the slow reshuffling between plays and then the quick sweet rush of the ball being snapped, the grit and the push of a run up the middle, the intricate ballet of a long bomb.

And above all, I love quarterbacks.

There's dashing Tom Brady, with the dimple in his chin and the crushed black velvet sports jacket he wears to press conferences, where he answers a frenzy of reporters' questions with his earnest "Aw, shucks, ma!" affect. At the other end of the spectrum is raffish Eli Manning, with his goofy grin and tousled locks that always seem to need a good combing. On the college side, you've got Texas Tech star Graham Harrell, with his cowboy twang and killer jaw line. Or USC's Mark Sanchez, who has thick black curls, penetrating eyes, and smooth dark skin.

Linemen are often bald and bulky and missing a few teeth. Fullbacks are inarticulate. Wide receivers are showstopper acrobats who hog the limelight. But quarterbacks (at least the best quarterbacks) earn their time in the sun. Their bodies are lean yet lined with muscle. When they speak, they choose their words sparingly and with care. They accept their celebrity in an offhand, almost grudging manner that in rare moments suggests grace.

They are patient, thoughtful, decisive, quick on their feet, steady yet comfortable improvising, and they have great hands. What more could you ask for in bed?

My love affair with football (and quarterbacks) goes back to my upbringing, in a home where football was a kind of religion. In fact, the demands of football often superceded those of religion. Once, when I asked my father how he could leave synagogue early on Yom Kippur to catch a big game on TV, he replied, "God will understand." Every year we paid for the privilege to subscribe to our season tickets (Section 44, row 71) at Michigan Stadium, and from the age of four, I accompanied the family to tailgate parties and games. Though I didn't really grasp the rules at first, I loved the pageantry of the bands, the cheerleaders, the buttons, the pom-

poms and pennants, the makeup and silly hats and outfits. In a way, it was an early introduction to the art of drag.

I also loved the atmosphere of freedom in a football stadium. In the suburb where I grew up, strangers and even acquaintances rarely acknowledged each other. At a football stadium, however, it was perfectly normal to accost someone while peeing side by side into a fifteen-foot-long metal trough to ask, "Can you believe that dumb call on third and three?" It was also normal for another of these men standing in a line with their dicks out on display to call out in response, "They ought to rape his ass!"

And strangely enough (though perhaps not coincidentally), for all its homophobia, the football stadium was that rare place where men, both on and off the field, felt free to touch each other, link arms, slap bodies, even hug for sheer, unabashed joy.

Finally, there were the players. As I grew older, I became aware that my interest in these well-built young men went beyond appreciation of their athletic skill and dexterity. In fact, I can safely credit a college football quarterback with my sexual awakening.

His name was Jim Harbaugh. I remember staring into his fierce yet kind brown eyes staring back at me from his photo in our glossy program. He had an easy smile and a stiff Roman nose, soft, feathered hair and a rugged jaw, a delicate neck and heavy shoulders. There was talk that he would make it in the pros.

Everyone I knew, adult and child, wanted to talk about Jim Harbaugh, though no one I knew had the answers to the questions I asked. What was he like? Who did he live with? What qualities was he looking for in a best friend? And, if I asked him nicely, would he take his shirt off for me?

In 1986 I was thirteen, and our mighty squad of Michigan Wolverines was scheduled to face off against the not-so-mighty Hawaii Rainbows. Being the kind of family that we were, we flew to Honolulu and made a vacation out of it. (I even got to miss a week of school.) One afternoon, we were on the beach in front of our hotel when we heard a commotion several feet away. It was our star quarterback, Jim Harbaugh, signing autographs and posing for pictures with fans with his dazzling steely smile.

He wasn't wearing a shirt, and his chest, smooth, rippled with soft taut curves, hairless, gleamed in the blazing Hawaiian sun. My head felt hot and strange. I was almost too scared to approach him, but someone stuck a pen, a notepad, and a camera in my hands, and I went.

He looked just like his picture in the football programs I kept in my nightstand, only better, younger, more solid. As I drew closer to the small crowd, I wished he'd chosen a skimpier bathing suit than his pair of knee-length navy blue cotton shorts with a little maize football on the left thigh. The shorts seemed to say: I'm not here to swim or sunbathe like common mortals. I'm here to shine among you briefly.

Soon it was my turn to have my picture taken with handsome Mr Harbaugh, who stood behind me, seemingly twice as tall as I was, his bare chest broad and bronzed, his face beaming. And then, as if he had a right to, he rested his heavy hands on my soft pale shoulders. I can still feel the warm, firm touch of those large, capable hands on my skin.

I'd never been touched by a man in this way, i.e., affectionately. I didn't even know men were capable of touching each other for the hell of it. I ached to move backwards a half-step closer to the rest of his body, to feel the weight of him nudging against my back, but I was frozen with fear and pleasure. Was this what life could be like always?

When I came back to my family, everyone congratulated me on the picture and the autograph, but as I watched Jim Harbaugh march down the beach, his tall, muscular figure getting smaller and smaller, I felt strangely let down. Take me with you, I wanted to beg. Touch my shoulders again. Keep me safe and warm in your room. Let me wait for you there at night and then we'll turn out the lights and I can whisper all my secrets softly in your ear.

Later, when I got home, I wrote him a letter, care of the Michigan athletic department. It began: "You probably don't remember me, but we met on the beach in Hawaii ..." After quizzing him about his life, I told him all about myself, my dreams of becoming a writer, of traveling around the world, my yearning to find someone who understood me.

Several weeks later, an envelope with unfamiliar handwriting and no return address arrived at our house. Inside was a piece of ruled paper torn from a notebook, inscribed with a half dozen sentences printed in neat capital letters.

Jim Harbaugh's letter to me began, thrillingly, "Aaron," and then, "Thank you for writing to me. It was nice to hear from you." He listed his major, his favorite hobbies, his roommates (three guys from the team), and told me, "When I'm with my friends, I am just myself. I try and give the same impression to reporters and fans." The note was signed with his team number, #4, beneath his name.

"Hang on to that letter," my brother advised. "It could be worth something someday." I needed no urging, though not because of the letter's potential cash value. I kept it with me all week and took it out and read it and reread it. And of course I immediately wrote back, care of the athletic department again. (How silly of Jim to forget to include a return address!) My plan was working. Jim Harbaugh was going to be my friend, and then he was going to invite me to come visit him in Ann Arbor, and then he'd touch me again, maybe even hug me. And once he realized how wonderful I was, he was going to ask me to live there with him, to be his roommate. They had high schools in Ann Arbor. I could go there while he finished his degree at U of M. And then if he got drafted by the NFL, I could follow him there too. My family might be upset at first, but they'd get used to the idea. Also, surely they'd see the advantages of living with a professional quarterback.

I mailed my letter. Then I waited. And waited. And waited.

I never did hear again from Jim Harbaugh, who didn't quite make it big in the pros, though he is now the coach of the Stanford Cardinal football team. I see him on ESPN sometimes. He's aged well, his body still trim, his face firmer but still handsome.

I hope he's doing well, and I'd like to extend my thanks for that first letter, and for that moment on the sun-kissed sands of Waikiki Beach when a thirteen-year-old boy's thoughts turned for the first time to desire.

McGinty Chapel

Martin Delacroix

Does God exist?

Let's assume He does. If you desperately need another guy's love, will the Lord help you get it?

I pondered these questions in 1962 when I worked as a counselor at a Methodist Youth Fellowship camp, a compound of dormitories and athletic fields, complete with a 500-seat sanctuary, swimming pool, and dining hall, all fronting Lake Griffin, a 16,000-acre, spring-fed body of water in central Florida. I'd come home from university for summer break, and the economy being what it was (lousy), no jobs were available for college students. Not in Cape Canaveral, anyway.

"Reverend Bostock said MYF's hiring," my mother told me. "I can put in a word."

She did, and I got interviewed, then employed. I took a Greyhound bus heading inland, leaving the coast behind.

I arrived at camp in late afternoon, just as the sun dipped behind the western tree line. Forty-foot tall leaf pines towered over much of the property, their dropped needles forming a rust-red carpet that muffled one's footfalls. The lake's banks were rimmed with bald cypress trees, spindly on top, hefty at their bases. Spanish moss hung from live oaks—monsters with spreading limbs. Some predated the Civil War, I later learned. A Leesburg resident, Angus McGinty, had donated land for the camp, and a cedar-shake chapel—a small structure with a cupola in lieu of a steeple—bore his name. It stood in a palmetto and pine forest, apart from the rest of campus, in a quiet spot where one could meditate undisturbed. You accessed McGinty Chapel via footpath, a trail barely wide enough for two people to pass.

My job wasn't difficult. I oversaw a dozen boys aged twelve to fourteen, making sure they ate and bathed and wrote home. I refereed flag football contests, umpired softball games. I took campers on canoe outings. I was Red Cross-certified as a lifeguard, and my primary duty was to staff the station at Lake Griffin's dock between breakfast and lunch. Each morning, after shepherding my kids to ceramics class or Bible study, I'd smear zinc oxide on my nose, squirt lemon juice on my hair (to keep it blond), and pull on my surfing baggies. I'd amble to the lake and plop into my elevated chair to daydream about Kirby Justice, a fellow male counselor.

Yeah, I was a gay boy. They called us "fruits" back then.

During my freshman year of college, almost two years before, I'd awakened in my bed at sun-up one day. My dorm mate, Avi Saperstein, a Jew from North Miami Beach, had pulled my dick out of my jockey shorts. Sucking away, he'd gotten me hard. I didn't try to stop him; it felt good. Plus, Avi was a decent-looking guy with dark eyes, wavy hair, and olive skin. He had a cute butt I'd admired when we showered down the hall. I patted the top of his head, whispering, "Don't stop," and after that we often shared a bed. He taught me how to suck cock and coaxed me into fucking him. I liked these activities. I told myself, "Okay, Martin, I guess this means you are queer."

Of course, in 1962 you didn't speak of such things; sex between men was taboo. If your friends found out you were gay, your life would be ruined. At best you'd be an outcast, at worst you'd get beat up, time and again.

Avi wasn't a good student, and he flunked out spring semester. When I returned to university in the fall, as a sophomore, I was alone in the sexual sense. I remained so throughout the school year, feeling isolated and miserable, spiritually starving to death.

Now, seated in my lifeguard station, shaded by a striped umbrella, I studied Kirby Justice's physique. A short distance from me, he taught a group of kids how to drain a swamped canoe, then right it and climb back aboard. His shoulders were broad and his waist was narrow. Gold streaks ran through his mop of brown hair, reflecting sunlight. Kirby majored in pre-law at Rollins College, a private institution in Winter Park. His family owned citrus groves in Indian River County, on Florida's southeastern coast, not far from where I had grown up. At home, he surfed Sebastian Inlet, the Sunshine State's premier break. His shoulder muscles looked like two shot puts rolling under his skin.

A few nights before, I'd shared a table with Kirby in the main dining hall. I told him I surfed myself, and he described what sorts of boards he owned. Each cost more than $300 (I knew this from reading *Surfer* magazine), while mine cost less than a hundred. Kirby belonged to the Christian Surfing Association, and over dinner he told me he often witnessed to other surfers he encountered on the line up, while they waited for waves.

I tried to imagine Kirby proselytizing with some Brevard County nitwit while the two bobbed on their boards in the Atlantic:

Kirby might say, "Have you accepted Christ as your savior?"

And the surfer might reply, "Look man, I'm here to catch a wave, nothing more. Keep that shit to yourself."

Thing was, I figured Kirby wouldn't get repulsed like I would if I tried tossing religion in some surfer's face. After all, Kirby had a patrician's bearing. An Inlet local, he was well-known. Guys probably listened without comment and went on about their surfing.

Something interesting happened the night I shared dinner with Kirby: our knees touched beneath the table. We both wore shorts and his leg hairs tickled mine. Kirby didn't withdraw his leg until several seconds had passed. This took place as we talked, and his eyes never left mine while the touching occurred.

Afterward, I asked myself if he had made a pass. But as the days went by, he sat with others. He did not acknowledge my presence in the dining hall or elsewhere, and I figured my queer imagination had gotten the best of me.

Unlike most camps, MYF did not require counselors to share sleeping quarters with their charges. We lived in separate buildings, sharing rooms with twin beds and hot plates and mini-refrigerators. My roommate was Kevin O'Bannon. An athletic guy my age, with red hair, freckles, and green eyes, he often lounged naked in our room. His meaty cock would roll about when he shifted position on his bed, studying a girlie magazine. He had several of these, along with pornographic paperbacks with titles like *Slave Niece* and *Tina in Bondage*, keeping them in a cardboard box under his bed. (Such publications were verboten under MYF policy, but Kevin was undeterred.) He said, "Screw the rules," and after lights-out he'd jack off, not subtly. His sheets rustled, his bed frame creaked, and his breath huffed as he climaxed. I was aroused just listening.

I never touched myself in our room at camp. I feared I might get caught by Kevin or someone else. I'd be branded a pervert and my sexual persuasion might become known.

I thought: Please, God, anything but that.

Back home and at college, I had masturbated chronically, always finding moments of solitude to pleasure myself, but now I had no privacy. During the day I lived amidst preachers and campers, fellow counselors and staff. At night, Kevin haunted our room. (He considered most everyone at camp "square" and did not participate in MYF social activities, preferring his magazines and books instead.)

My sexual tension mounted. Twice I had wet dreams, soaking my underwear. As weeks passed, I became infatuated with Kirby Justice. I loved his aquamarine eyes, his dimpled chin, and furry legs. I admired the line of hair descending from his navel into his surfing shorts, and I adored the scent of the aftershave he used—Aqua Velva.

Sadly, I wasn't alone in my feelings. Female counselors swarmed Kirby, flirting and maneuvering for seats near his during mealtimes. One girl, Andrea Nips (no joke), gained the upper hand as we entered the month of July. Before supper, she and Kirby would rendezvous, and they'd enter the dining hall together. Of course, the two never held hands (public displays of affection were forbidden between MYF counselors), but I sensed something carnal between them. Sometimes, during dinner, I'd catch them grinning as if they shared a delicious secret.

Sunday, Tuesday, and Thursday evenings I was free of responsibility. I could do as I pleased—play cards in the rec hall or take a moonlight canoe excursion on the lake. I could watch television in the lounge in my dormitory. I could do anything, really, but masturbate—the thing I wanted most to do.

On a Tuesday evening in mid-July, Kevin lay naked upon his bed, reading a Harold Robbins novel, *The Carpetbaggers* (another publication beneath MYF standards). The air in our room felt sticky and warm. A box fan hummed in the window, fluttering the pages of a movie magazine I was reading. I admired a full-page photograph of Richard Chamberlain, a sexy television actor. (What cheekbones!) I wondered what he'd look like naked. My eyes traveled to Kevin's cock, then back to Chamberlain's photo, and my penis stirred inside my Bermuda shorts. I slipped into my sandals and T-shirt, telling Kevin I would take a walk. I shoved a hanky into my pocket.

Outside, the air was still, but cooler. Fireflies darted about. A three-quarter moon silvered treetops. Inside camper dormitories, lights shone and kids' voices spilled from the windows. They played cards or board games in their pajamas, swapping stories. Their laughter punched across campus, irritating me to no end. Pine sap and freshly fallen needles scented the air with a sour aroma. I walked to the lake, hoping I'd find solitude, but a group of counselors, a mix of boys and girls, sat in a circle under a dock light, sipping from soda bottles and chattering away.

I turned on my heel and left before they noticed my presence.

Where could I go to be alone?

I glanced at my wristwatch's radium dial and McGinty Chapel came to mind. Who'd be there at nine p.m.? Would the door be locked?

Leaving behind the dining hall and other campus buildings, I soon heard nothing but crickets chirping. I came to the chapel path. It bisected a bank of saw palmettos and moonlight reflected off the shrubs' waxy fronds.

I glanced here and there. No one around.

Drawing a breath, I strode down the path, listening to needles crunch under my feet. Slash pines cast shadows. The trail meandered, it rose and fell, and twice I tripped over exposed tree roots. Things were so quiet I heard my own breathing. I told myself, "Alone at last. You're finally—"

Noises came from ahead. Someone brushed against palmettos, advancing toward me.

Shit!

Stepping off the path, I took care to be quiet when I parted fronds. Crouching behind a slash pine, I raised my chin to peer out. It was Andrea Nips. Her arms were crossed beneath her breasts and her gaze was focused on the footpath. Her sleeveless blouse glowed in the moonlight as she made her way toward campus. She passed within five feet of me, and I was able to see her facial expression. Her lips were drawn tight against her teeth, her forehead was furrowed, and a tear glistened on her cheek.

Had she spoken with God in the chapel? Had she shared her deepest thoughts?

I counted to 100 before I emerged. The chapel stood in a clearing, a modest, rectangular structure with double-hung windows on both flanks and a peaked roof. Three steps led to a landing, to a coffered door sheltered by a cedar-shake awning. A yellow bug bulb burned in a fixture beside the door, casting a cone of light. The chapel's interior was dark.

I climbed the steps, sandals slapping my heels. Clutching the doorknob, I gave it a twist and the door swung into the sanctuary, hinges sighing like a pair of satiated lovers.

I peered inside, letting my eyes adjust to the dimness. Moonlight slanted in through windows to my left. The corners of the chapel were dark as tar, but elsewhere I saw outlines of things. A half dozen pews offered seating. Up front, on a raised platform, a metal cross and a pair of candlesticks perched upon a table draped with an altar cloth. A row of books—Bibles or hymnals—occupied a wall shelf. An upright piano faced another wall. The room had no ceiling and the roof beams and rafters were exposed. Above the altar a stained-glass window glistened in the moonlight, depicting Christ in the Garden of Gethsemane. The room smelled of burnt wax and mildew.

I closed the door, then sat before the altar in a pew, looking at Jesus. I rested my hands in my lap. Closing my eyes, I thought of Kevin O'Bannon, of Kirby Justice, of Avi Saperstein. I even thought about Richard Chamberlain. My cock grew stiff and I unzipped my shorts, producing my erection. I stroked myself, but despite my sexual arousal, sadness crept through me. Was I condemned to live a life without love? Without sex? Would my days be dull and dry as cake flour? Why had the Lord made me queer?

My eyes watered and tears tickled my cheeks. I sank to my knees before the altar and my cock bobbed before me. Joining my hands before my chest, I interlaced my fingers. I whispered, "God, if You hear me, will You please help me? I can't live this way. I need a man's love, I need his touch. I know it's wrong, but—"

A floorboard creaked behind me.

I froze and my scalp prickled. Who was there? I was too frightened to turn and look. I remained on my knees, cock pointing at the ceiling. My pulse drummed inside my head.

Footfalls sounded, grew louder. I held my breath as long as I could, then I exhaled. My nose crinkled and my head tilted to one side and I thought, wait a second, I know that scent. It's … Aqua Velva.

Kirby knelt beside me and the floorboards creaked anew. He reached for my cock. Taking it in his fingers, he examined it while a pearl of pre-cum oozed from the tip, reflecting moonlight. He unzipped his shorts and produced his own erection, one with a head shaped like a plum. He took my hand and placed it on his dick. I squeezed him. Bringing his lips to my ear, he whispered, "Shall we pray, Martin?"

I nodded and we commenced stroking each other, eyes on the altar.

We spoke in unison, "Our Father, who art in heaven, hallowed be Thy name ..."

When we reached the Prayer's "power and glory" part, Kirby and I experienced a glory all our own. Our jizz dotted the chapel's pine floor.

I haven't attended church in forty years.

People sometimes ask me, "Do you believe in God?"

Logic dictates a negative response. If God exists, why can't we see Him? And why would He let such awful things happen? How does one explain the Holocaust? Why do tsunamis kill tens of thousands of people?

Religion doesn't make sense, I know. But I had my moment with Kirby Justice. Several, in fact, before summer ended.

God heard my prayer in McGinty Chapel, I am certain of it.

I tell people, "Sure, I have faith. The Lord's here for you if you believe in Him."

That's what I think, anyways.

Just a Phase

S. Bear Bergman

For the record, it's really as simple as this: I wanted to have sex. In some measure, I wanted to be having fond and tender sex; in other ways I craved rough and dirty sex. But at sixteen, like pretty much every sixteen-year-old in the history of puberty, I was prepared to take what I could get. Especially me, big and awkward as I was or at least felt at the time, I would take what I could get. And girls—girls were willing to have sex with me. They wanted to. Girls were smart and cute and smelled nice, so that seemed like a fine plan, and suddenly somehow I was a dyke and only dating girls, which certain people to whom I was related fervently hoped would turn out to be Just A Phase. And lo—they were right. The fact that I was living as a girl also turned out to be a phase, a turn of events that I don't imagine anyone was really expecting. But such is the way of wishes, I hear. It behooves a wisher to be very, very specific about what they wish for.

I like girls. I always have, and I appreciate femmes in particular for their many fabulous ways and particular skills, not the least of which is and has been making me feel like I am just 'zactly the right thing in a world that fairly regularly has taken time to tell me I'm a fuckup, a freak, or some other kind of disaster. Femmes, in addition to being savvy and sassy and generally elsewise charming, stood each of those accusations on its head for me. Through femme eyes, my masculine ways were desirable, my urges and impulses toward chivalry were admirable. My fear and shame about my fat and ungainly body, and my utter disinterest in revealing it to others, were re-imagined for me as the understandable reluctance of the stone butch to make myself vulnerable. To go with it, femmes attributed to me the admirable value of prioritizing the satisfaction of a woman. Considering that boys generally took the time to yell unpleasant things at me out of car windows and otherwise ignored me entirely, this seemed like a spectacular upgrade, and one for which I was very grateful.

But I never stopped liking boys. I came out, when I came out that first time, as bisexual. In the fullness of time I revised that to queer, because I had learned some new theories about sex and gender, and gained more understanding of my particular desires (as well as some new and frankly exciting things about acting them out). But it took me until I was in my mid twenties to start thinking again about men, and sex, as something that might happen for me.

In part, this waffling and misdirection with regard to my sexuality was a failure of modeling. It was some time before I was grown enough to meet people who wore their complex sexualities in full array. Longer still, I think, until I was able to move through my hormone-driven, want-want, right-now phase and recognize what I was responding to in my sexual partners. I liked, and continue to like, queers and freaks and outlaws. I like transgressive genders and transgressive sexualities, especially in people whose expression of those things has a lot of whimsy, and when someone's sex and gender cues are all shook up I like that even better. As you might imagine, this is hard to articulate as a teenager (and was even more difficult twenty years ago, before the magical Internet swept in and normalized so many kinds of desire that had previously been served only by fervid imagination and limp mimeographed newsletters sent in plain wrappings). I like expressive, entitled sexuality; a cocktail of thoughtful gender expression and feminist sensibility. Show me someone who has examined cultural gender norms and cherry-picked exactly which of those things suit hir, and is serving them back with a certain style and a come-hither-or-fuck-off attitude, and I will show you someone with whom I could cheerfully pass at least a sweaty afternoon.

But there's this other issue, too. I like boys. Well, really, what I like is masculinity, and what sort of genital or bodily topography it comes with is definitely of interest, but not a limiting factor. There is a theory-enriched scholarly office in my brain patiently telling me that each and every one of the things I like about masculinity—sweat, fur, muscles, a certain fix-it attitude, authority, neckties—could also be embodied by the femininely gendered. This is true, and the femininely gendered people I have felt great desire for in my lifetime have all had, or had been, at least some of those things in their own inimitable femme ways. But the more I allow myself to embody and enjoy my own natural masculinity—the more I move toward my most comfortable (if complicated) places of my own gender expression—the more I find myself interested in those (and other) traits in their masculine forms.

This has caused some issues, and not just because I am the author of a book entitled *Butch Is a Noun* in which I talk quite a lot about femmes. I don't really know how to explain what happened. I was never lying. I liked, and continue to like, girls—and especially femmes, for whom I have so very much esteem. I love the tender, brilliant dance of butch and femme, the ways that femmes have soothed and do soothe some of my most tender places (and excite some of the others). Inexorably, though, the needle on the compass of my desires has been remagnetized, and now swings toward the bulk and woof of boys, even though so many other tastes remain the same: I still fall like a ton of bricks for the smartypantses, the storytellers, the activists. I still like bigger bodies, and remain fairly well convinced that there is no such thing as too much ass.

And yet, somehow, and with not a lot of warning, the more I moved toward masculinity, the more I wanted it. I know that I am not the only one this happens to, not the only masculinely gendered, female-bodied being who has suddenly been startled to discover, while buying cute boxer briefs, that ze was also lewdly imagining how some cute boy would look in them.

The adjustment hasn't been so difficult for me—I always liked

boys, I could just never figure out how to go about that, as a puta-
tive lesbian. The fallout, however, has been substantial. The end
of my first marriage eventually turned out to be, in part, because
my fantastic femme wife no longer felt as though she wanted to be
married to someone essentially living in so many ways as a faggot. While I have since remarried and adore my husband—and am
reveling, even as I type this exact sentence, in fresh newlywed love
with him squashed up against me on a plane—I regret that my ex-
wife eventually felt devalued and unappreciated. A bitter harvest
indeed for someone who did a great deal to redeem me from the
nay-saying monsters in my own brain. It wasn't what I would have
preferred.

And so now, I live mostly as a fag. I have fashion glasses and I put
product in my hair and I am extra thoughtful about the housewares
and I do unspeakable, delicious things with the other fellas when
I get the chance (which is also complicated, since I am not in any
way a Man, but luckily there are other queers who are queer for
queers like me, and we manage pretty well together). I treasure the
quantum femmes in my life who can still make me blush, can tune
me up into my best butch behavior with a raise of the eyebrow or
a certain, complicated smile—and I serve them as best I am able,
somehow better because I feel fully seen by them. The husband and
I, we have them for brunch. I am always stirred to better locution,
better manners, and better outfits by them—but not to heights of
sexual desire, most of the time (there are a few lifetime exceptions
to this rule).

And so it turns out that my mother and other relatives were
right, and I was entirely wrong. Liking girls was just a phase I
passed through. I indulged myself in it for a while, when it worked
well for me, but once I was older my preferences naturally aligned
themselves toward the company of men, and I eventually married
a Nice Jewish Boy with whom to make babies. All of that, all those
half-realized wishes made when someone thought I couldn't see or
hear, turned out to be true.

Oddly, however, no one to whom I am related seems to be much placated by this change. I don't know why. It's exactly what they wanted.

A Walk around Eros

Tim Miller

I met Alistair in London when I was performing at the Institute of Contemporary Art in 1994. The ICA occupies a building that looks like an extravagant wedding cake hunkering at the end of the Mall. It was built for the Royal Stables, then served as the German embassy, and today cradles galleries and a performance space—the end product of an ascending (some would say descending) trajectory from horses to Germans to artists.

I had been staying for a week with my friend Richard in Ladbroke Grove. We had enjoyed a sweet romance when I was performing in Sydney the year before. With his sexy swagger, Richard had been voted Person Most Likely to Get Rimmed at Oxford. But because I was now doing a workshop at the ICA, I had been rewarded with two hotel nights in South Kensington off Cromwell Road, so I had relocated.

I arrived at the ICA early to lead my gay men's performance workshop. Gliding up the ornate stairway to the meeting rooms, I could hear from far below the clip-clop of feet coming up the stairs. I greeted every guy as he entered, began to connect the specific name with the specific nose piercing (there were six Simons and two septum rings). One man told me he had just come out two months before. Another said his lover had died of AIDS the previous week. One man was a famous choreographer in the UK who would make some of the participants nervous. Just before it was time to begin, I slid down the banister to the bathroom on the floor below to take a pee. I heard a new set of footsteps coming up the stairs. I peeked down. There he was, walking up the stairs—a gorgeous neo-Celtic grunge boy.

He had that wonderful, slightly shocked Scots-Irish nineteenth-century look, like those old daguerreotype photos of the fresh-faced Civil War soldiers of both sides, so optimistic about their big adventure before they got slaughtered at Antietam or Chickamauga. This look on the alternative-styled queer boy made him exactly the kind of young man Walt Whitman would favor on his shifts as a nurse back at the Civil War hospital. Old Walt would have given many lingering thigh massages to such a youth.

"Hi," I said.

"Oh, hello," he replied, seeming to look around for a possible route of escape.

He looked nervous. He had the alertness and the terror of a sleek animal during hunting season. It seemed like he didn't know what to say next.

"Well, thanks for coming. I'm Tim."

"I'm Alistair."

He pronounced the last syllable of his name so that it rhymed with hair. Speaking of hair, his had been cut recently, approximating the standard London short faggot do. He was tall and skinny in his grunge-rock splendor. We shook hands. A buzz moved through me, as if I'd stuck a fork in a light socket. Our hands held each other and we saw the future. I saw a kiss in a bus station in Scotland. I saw us fucking each other a thousand times and then once more. I saw a tearful parting in Pittsburgh International Airport. I saw hours of long-distance phone calls. I saw hearts that might open to each other. I saw the impossibility of the situation becoming possible. Then the room came back into view.

Sensing an unusual accent even for England, I asked him, "Where are you from?"

"I'm from Western Australia. I grew up in Perth, the world's most isolated industrialized city. I just finished Uni."

Uh-oh. Down under. This might be the beginning of a little

journey to the underworld. A journey that I had been postponing for some time.

"Shall we go up?" I asked.

I jumped right into the workshop with this group of English, Scottish, Australian, and French faggots. The men in the group did honest and metaphor-rich pieces about the feelings and energies that dwelt in their bodies, their assholes, love handles, and palms. Alistair, who I was watching very carefully throughout the workshop, did a haunting chanting piece about his throat as a place of power and expression. It gave me a boner.

The workshop ended. In a loud mob we retreated down the stairs to the ICA bar. I approached Alistair, who was pretending to order a drink.

"Did you enjoy the workshop?"

"Oh, yeah," Alistair said, very enthusiastically.

Nonchalantly I sipped my pint of lager, which the barman had begrudgingly slid down the bar to me.

I manufactured a big performative yawn and said, "Well, I'm going to get going pretty soon."

Alistair didn't miss a beat. "Yeah, I should go too before the Tube closes."

We walked onto the Mall and crunched over the crackly gravel through Admiralty Arch. I knew we had just missed the last train for the night, so Alistair would have to take the night bus on Trafalgar Square to get home.

Instead, we walked up past the night bus stand and then up Charing Cross Road and over on Shaftsbury. I felt a compulsion this particular night to spend some time with this young man from Perth. What would it take to lure him into my bed? What would happen to me if he said yes?

We got to Piccadilly Circus and crossed over to the statue of Eros without getting killed by the boomeranging taxicabs. (The Australianisms are already creeping in!)

Alistair and I walked around the statue. As always, I looked at its perfect ass and wanted to climb up to feel the smooth bronze muscle of the polished butt. It was getting late. Because of my hotel room, we had somewhere to go.

"Would you like to hop in a cab and come back to South Kensington, and we could hang out at my hotel room?" I asked, much more nervous than I let on.

"Oh, ta. Yeah. That'd be quite nice," Alistair said. Then, so he could be sure I had heard his soft-spoken voice, he said more loudly, "Yes."

We got out of the cab at the Gloucester Road Tube station, so I could buy a late night sweet and milk, and strolled down Cromwell Road to the Adelphi Hotel. I am tempted now to start using UK-ish words like lorry and singlet and gym boots in a sentence such as, "The lorry laden with milk for morning shook the ground of Cromwell Road under our plodding gym boots as Alistair and I walked toward Hotel Fate, our sweaty summer singlets sticking to our expectant skin."

But I will resist that temptation. As we walked into the lobby of the Adelphi Hotel, the Indian night clerk gave me a dirty look that seemed to say, "I have to stay up all night to make money for my family in South London and let in poofters with their trade to fuck on the sheets that my cousin will rip off of their bed tomorrow and have to scrub the cum out of." I thought he was almost going to protest my bringing a young man back to this fine establishment, in spite of the water damage in every room, but he seemed to decide that Alistair was harmless and handed me my key.

We went up the once-plush stairs and into my tiny room, which did have a toilet at least. We sat on the bed and ate the just-purchased cookies—"bikkies," Alistair called them. Chatting about Australia and what it was like to be foreigners in London, we lounged close to each other. While talking about Protestant and Catholic stuff, Alistair told me that he had chosen Saint Sebastian as his patron saint during his catechism. This truly bizarre piece of autobiography told me it was time to make a move.

I rolled my head against Alistair's chest. Up and over his collarbone went my lips until we began to kiss. I felt quite peaceful. I was sitting down to a meal that would go on for years, a meal with a loaves-and-fishes feeling to it. In that spark of desire was a renewable resource that would keep feeding us for some time. We didn't need to have "great sex" right then. What was clear to me at that moment was that the raw materials were there, the frame of a building that might one day be able to provide some shelter. Alistair and I felt one another's skin through our clothes. I saw his body, long and skinny and full of life.

I loosened his hanging-by-a-thread worn-out leather belt and let his pants fall to the floor as we tumbled onto the bed. The sizzling heat in the hotel room blew out the top of the thermometer at this point.

Alistair and I were now launched on a high-drama, high-wire, high-stakes romance. The excitement started before we had even woken up the next day. As we slept, that early morning, a bomb went off at the Israeli consulate a few blocks away.

"What was that?" I groggily asked, groping my way up from a sweaty summer sleep.

Alistair didn't stir. Instead he made an enormous sound as he ground his teeth and then shifted over onto his stomach. This maneuver took particular effort, almost as if he were lifting a great weight in his dream. I peeked at him lying there in his naked skin, the single sheet tossed away during our fitful night's rest. The flimsy curtains didn't block out much of the sun, which avalanched into the room on the hottest day of the brief English summer. Looking at the sleeping Alistair, I saw his man's torso just starting to peek out from his alternative-queer-boy/Dickensian-workhouse-waif chest. Years later this would be something I would tease him about after he discovered the gym and acquired his muscles.

"When I met you, you looked like this …" I would say, making my shoulders and chest all concave and Little Nell-ish.

In the oddly hot sun on that first morning, I let my fingers slip down the long slalom from his slender shoulders to the hollow of his lower back, a little hair sprouting there in that wild animal spot. I rubbed the base of his spine in wider and wider circles. I kneaded the steep ascent up Alistair's ass, which, along with his heart, was the most developed part of his body. It was full and muscular under my hand as the cheeks rose and fell a tiny bit with each breath. My hand circled his butt, as if I were a penny arcade fortuneteller rubbing a crystal ball, hoping for a sneak preview of the future. My hand rested on his sweet behind. I fell back to sleep as the second bomb exploded.

Unbeknownst to us, while we slept together that first time in my hotel in South Kensington, strange events were taking place. Alistair's ex-boyfriend, Phil, who, as is so often the case, was not quite as ex as Alistair had led me to believe, had gone to the police and reported Alistair missing. The Institute for Contemporary Art received calls from the authorities about a young Australian who had been kidnapped from a Gay Men's Performance Workshop. Phil had given the police a photograph, and they were walking the sex-beats of Hampstead Heath, asking if anyone had seen this man, Alistair McCartney. Fortunately, they had not yet begun dredging the Men's Pond when Alistair finally returned home later that morning to Kentish Town. Phil's fury was immediately unleashed and Alistair had to endure an inquisition of shame.

I had checked out of the hotel and was now back at Richard's. Since Alistair and I had nowhere private to get naked, we didn't get to have full bed-sex again, though we did mess around some in the ICA dressing room when I put him in the show as the extra performer who washes my naked body. (You have to love performance art.) So we spent my remaining days in London taking chaste walks together around Eros. Like teenagers without anywhere to go, we courted each other as the accumulation of desire built up. While we talked about everything we needed to cover, we used these monastic walks as a good way to discover what existed between us.

The night before I left London, Alistair walked me to the

136 · *I Like it Like That*

Piccadilly Tube to say good-bye. Dodging the usual wandering herds of drunken football hooligans pissing and vomiting in the street—ah, romantic London—we fell into a sharpened awkward silence.

"Alistair," I said, deciding I was ready to launch a possibility, like a frail paper boat into a stiff current, "I'm going to be doing a queer men's project up in Scotland in a couple of months. Maybe you could come up and visit me in Glasgow."

"Yeah," he replied with a careful suppression of enthusiasm, a lesson he had probably learned well as a child as a means of avoiding disappointment. "I would like that."

We kissed under the statue—a pact, a contract, a wedding in a way, the first of many we would share: Moving in Together. Getting Tested. Getting a Dog—and then we held hands and walked around and around Eros. Our feet stirred up dirt, dust, molecules—a swirling tornado around the statue … well, this always happens in dream sequences!

The love and desire that rose up from that one hotel bed in London followed our footpath around Eros. Like a tidal wave rising from the sea, it would flood down Regent Street, across the Mall toward Buckingham Palace, fill the Thames and wash all the way to America, California, Venice Beach. Our love would bring us to the shore of a western sea, where we have made our home, and our love would confront the ugly crap of America's immigration laws. We were ready to claim our space, our love, our bed. Our country.

Stroke of Fate

Jeffrey Rotin

There's a guy at my gym who I find irresistible, even though I think he's an insufferable bore and kind of funny looking. It took me a while to figure out why I always feel the stirrings of an erection every time I talk to him, even as I surveyed the awkward propor-tions of his body and wondered when, please God, he'd stop talking about his master's thesis on ants.

It's his physical touch.

Sometimes, to make a point as he's talking, he'll casually place his palm on my chest or graze his fingers down my arm. When he gets really animated, he'll grab my shoulders. At first I figured it was simply his Italian blood, his expressive way of talking with his hands. Then I realized it's deliberate.

His hands on my skin—he always makes contact with bare skin—are like warm scotch flowing through my body. My reserve melts, my defenses drop. And I always think, wow, he'd be amazing in bed.

What's more amazing, though, is that these encounters stand out as such isolated occurrences. In sexual situations, men rarely ex-plore my body. Predictably, most zero in on my mouth and crotch. Maybe the tease of an occasional tweaked nipple or a nibble on my neck. Woohoo. The rest of my body—toned arms, slightly furry chest, lean torso, firm inner thighs—remains uncharted territory. That these body parts escape attention remains an ongoing source of bewilderment and disappointment.

It's not narcissism—I'm not looking for body worship. It's about sensual gratification. It's about what gets me really worked up, pushes me over the edge. I like to caress other men's bodies, too, trace my hand along their warm skin, feel the contrast of hard and soft contours. But they rarely pick up on my cues and follow suit. And I'll be lying there thinking: *What am I, a leper? Run your hands over my body, goddamn it.*

True, I could simply ask my sexual partners to touch me, but it's not the same. I like it to be spontaneous, a surprise. If I have to explain what I want, the pleasure is diminished. I know I'm being unreasonable, but that's just the way it's been—ever since my appointment with Dr L.

I was a somewhat inexperienced twenty-one-year-old. I'd been having sex with guys for about two years. When I couldn't shake a nagging virus, I went to a local walk-in clinic.

The clinic was like a second-hand garment: faded, worn out, and fraying at the edges. The linoleum floor was a patchwork of nicks and scuff marks. The top of the receptionist's wooden desk was darkened and oily from the thousands of patients like me who had placed their clammy palms on it.

The receptionist said I could see Dr L right away and pointed to a waiting area down the hall. I slunk down into a cracked orange vinyl chair in the windowless waiting area. A static-filled Muzak version of the Carpenters' "Close to You" droned through the loud-speaker system.

I noted two doctors in this area of the clinic: one was a fat, pasty middle-aged man with limp strands of hair across the top of his head. The other was young, tanned, and gorgeous. With my luck, I sighed, my doctor will be the ugly one. I grabbed a magazine.

Then I heard my name called. I took a deep breath and looked up. It was the gorgeous doctor.

He had matinee-idol good looks: short, blond sun-bleached hair, tennis-tanned skin, and a winsome smile that exposed flawless white teeth. I followed him into his office and studied the graceful movement of his chiseled body, barely concealed underneath a snug-fitting Polo top and cream-colored linen pants. And loafers without socks. How undoctor-like, I mused.

He was surprisingly chatty and easygoing. And decidedly un-clinical. I had the delicious impression of being examined by the captain of the varsity football team. I pegged him at his late twenties at the most. Probably an intern.

I tried my best to answer all his questions, but my attention kept wandering—to his expressive blue eyes, his full lips, the outline of his chest, his strong hands. Even his bare ankles were beautiful. I tried to imagine his naked body.

He asked me to step up to the exam table, whereupon he began a routine checkup. He had an awkward eagerness that I had never witnessed before in a doctor. When I gagged from the dryness of the wooden tongue depressor, which he applied with all the gentleness of a linebacker, he nervously apologized.

Then he instructed me to lie down. He slowly pulled my cashmere sweater up to my chest and began pressing on my stomach. I wasn't entirely sure what he was doing, and wasn't certain if he knew either, but frankly, I didn't care.

Then he did the most remarkable thing. Instead of telling me to lower my trousers, as doctors typically do, he undid my belt, unzipped my fly, and pulled my jeans down to mid-thigh level. He slipped his hand under my briefs.

He had also forgotten to put on rubber gloves.

"Breathe," he said, as he pressed on my groin, his fingers grazing my pubic hair. Staring blankly into the fluorescent lights on the ceiling, I gasped with a slight intake of air, and held it. My brain hit a panic button. Was it wrong to be enjoying this?

"Breathe," he repeated. Lying there passively and exposed, with my sweater hiked up to here and my pants yanked down to there, with the warmth of his hands on my skin, the best I could muster was a wheeze as the panic signal transmitted throughout my body. My skin was tingling and sweaty, sticking to the paper cover of the exam table.

"Breathe," he said again, his fingers continuing to press down around my groin. My eyes rolled back in my head as every nerve ending in my body responded with a wave of exclamation marks.

"And again," he said, oblivious to the fact that I was starting to hyperventilate. I was feeling woozy. I was also getting an erection, which I warded off by directing my thoughts elsewhere. The national anthem. Earthquakes. Cancer. *God Save the Queen*. The Queen taking a crap.

When the exam was over, I slipped off the table and stood on the floor, exhausted. I felt like I just had sex. Incredible sex. Even though he hadn't touched my dick and I hadn't climaxed.

It was a revelation.

The incident might have been relegated to a sordid doctor fetish, but a few months later a boyfriend sealed my fate when, on our first night together, he gently stroked and kissed the sides of my torso. Again, small firecrackers exploded in every nerve ending of my body. Drove me wild. I was hooked.

After that, guys would be mystified when I insisted I was more into foreplay and I didn't necessarily have to orgasm with them. I do a pretty good job of that on my own. And while the sensation of my dick in an orifice is fantastic, after all these years it's become a bit, well, *routine*. When the tactile element isn't there, I can lose interest pretty quickly.

I scan my memory for occasions when sexual partners have spontaneously explored my body through erotic touch, and sadly, only a few examples immediately spring to mind. A wild fling from years ago, who had an inventive way of giving massages using whatever was at hand: a feather, the pages of a book, a necklace, the spiky tips of his hair. A bisexual dancer from Seattle who wasn't into oral or anal sex, or even kissing another guy for that matter, and kept wrestling me for the upper hand until finally we simply stroked each other's bodies (the no kissing part was the deal breaker). A friend at a radical faerie gathering who insisted I lay back, close my eyes, and do nothing while he ran his hands over me.

Ah, there's the rub. Sometimes I'm betrayed by my own aggressive impulses—the need to put on a performance—and my inability to allow someone to reciprocate. I like to be in the driver's seat, and my default position is to do all the work. I am my own undoing.

I've considered Body Electric workshops where I could explore the art of non-sexual erotic touch with other men. But that seems too much like asking for it. It needs to be unprompted. I'm also a bit of a prude about having strangers paw me. Hey, I never claimed I was easy to please.

But sometimes it all comes together. Like the guy at the gym. I bumped into him in the sauna the other day. It was just the two of us. When I complained that my legs were sore from a tough workout, he moved next to me and, without saying a word, massaged my calves and feet. When he finished, I thanked him with a gentle stroke of my hand down his chest. Soft Mediterranean skin. Mmmm.

After, in the locker room, I gave him my phone number. I want to hear more about those ants.

The Daddyhunt Follies

Don Shewey

July 6: I had a good conversation over dinner with my friend Michael about what makes sex satisfying. For him, it's either passionate abandon or long, leisurely languor that allows him to let go of being in charge. For me, it has to do with feeling relaxed and free to be myself. I realize that's the benefit of a long-term relationship for me—the easy intimacy of knowing each other, having a shared vocabulary, the shorthand of key words, familiar gestures, favorite meals. Of course, over the long haul, the familiar can go rancid and stale. But when the relationship is over and I'm out in the cold shivering, that familiarity looks pretty damn good. And having tasted it, inevitably I long to plunge deep into that intimacy with someone new, an impossible but irresistible quest.

Since I broke up with Patrick in March, I've had too many hasty, meaningless blowjobs, not enough spiritual communion. I've spent a lot of time cruising for sex, checking email, in pursuit. And when I do have sex, it tends to be fast and paltry. What can I do to shift that? Start with massage exchange. Introduce kinky play (blindfolds, restraints). Only play with guys I'm really hot for, who are smart, who can talk. Sacrifice short-term pleasure (blowjobs) for bigger goals and gains (Saturday night sleepover).

Today, for the first time in a long time, I felt tired of New York City and experienced it as dirty and grungy and ugly. I need a break. But where? Fort Lauderdale? P-Town? (Fire Island doesn't feel like enough of a getaway.) San Diego? Las Vegas?

July 10: On *Daddyhunt.com*, a flurry of IMs and emails with a handsome, furry-faced lad in San Diego named Miguel, exchange of pix, escalating quickly to an invitation to visit.

dadscub wrote: Don, Just wanted to tell you that I just checked ticket prices online and they are not that bad right now, around $360 round trip. I would be happy to split the bill with you also. Seriously. Tell me what you think. Would love to have a handsome hairy Dad in my bed ... Hug, Miguel

hairybeast wrote: dang, Miguel, great minds thinking alike! i've just been checking out airline prices too. and reading yr email gives me a boner, for some strange reason ... :--) lemme ponder all this. i like yr eagerness—good quality for a cub! Don

dc: Hey, if you have any more pics of your hairy self ... send 'em to me. Your pics bone me up good! Hug, M.

hb: woof woof and triple woof! RIP. i like seeing familiar sites in yr pix—Black's Beach, my favorite on earth! and Yucca Valley, where I did a powerful meditation/breathwork retreat in 1993 or '94. p.s.: more pix of me to come

dc: Glad to hear that you are familiar with the same spots I go to. Ever been to Cuyamaca Falls? About 30 minutes east of here. I'll take you there if you have not been.

hb: nope, never been to Cuyamaca Falls—sounds like a good road trip to me. i'm weighing August 2–6 but that would be a 4-night stay, and you know what they say about house guests being like fish ... as we just learned in my Italian class, *dopo tre giorni puzza*.- i'm liking this idea, but it's also way wacky, considering how little we know about each other ...!

dc: I got your pics. NICE. The one of you standing in the woods just knocked my socks off. It's my desktop wallpaper now. WHUUFFF You are way too much my type. As for the possible awkwardness of your visiting, well, I plan to show you the guest room, and you can set up camp there. I'll give you a key to the house, too. That way, in the event that our chemistry is not total nuclear fireworks, you won't feel in the way, obligated, or tied down in any way. Heck, I would not be offended if you had another date planned during your stay. I am far from a possessive person, especially at this point in our getting to know each other! I hope my overly realistic view on all this is not a turnoff.

hb: thanks for your great email. you absolutely took words out of my mouth about the uncertainty of meeting. your directness is totally appealing and admirable to me. i wuz gonna say some version of the same thing, and worried about being too blunt. i'm with you 100 % on the realities of a first-time visit. i'll give u a buzz this evening and see how it goes voice to voice. i'm not one for long phone conversations, i much prefer face to face (body to body, etc.), but ya gotta start somewhere, eh? bi fur now, Don

dc: Man, those outdoor boner shots get me every time. I blew a load about an hour ago to the one you sent me yesterday. You're too much. Yeah, I am not big on phone conversations in general, not even with people I know well. I do want to hear your voice at least once though. We can just talk about the weather for 2 minutes or something. Ha ha. Hugs, M

hb: LOL—mutual. the one of you that gets me going is the "Skinny Dipping" one. i guess we're both Naked Outdoors kinda guys, eh? XO, Don

dc: yeah, I am a total nature boy nudist. I love hiking around Palm Springs with nothing but my hiking boots and backpack. The skinny dipping picture was taken at Cuyamaca Falls, by the way. I'll definitely be taking you there for some action in the sun. Big Hugs, Miguel

July 15: I met Marta at the Museum of Modern Art and she encouraged me to go ahead and have the San Diego adventure. My therapist said it didn't matter if I go or not, but whatever choice I make, do it responsibly—choose what I'm doing. So I went ahead and booked the flight. What I'm choosing is a four-day date, an experiment in continuous intimacy with someone I don't know. Instant gratification? Perhaps. It's also an effort to kick-start my dating regimen, so I'm not quite so particular and demanding here at home. Miguel is overjoyed that I'm coming. I inquired about his serostatus (positive, as I'd guessed). He's a smoker, and he's aware that smoking is on my "not wanted" list.

July 16: Yeesh, am I learning the hard way how to meet potential dates and fuck buddies. Now I've definitively learned: don't meet complete strangers for a full meal first. Today I knew as soon as I laid eyes on Paul, a block away, that I wasn't attracted to him, so sitting through an hour and a half of theater talk was agonizing. I overate out of nervousness. He really wanted to take me home. I said not tonight. He said, can I see you again? I said I don't feel a physical connection. He became practically hysterical. What did I say, was I too open, I feel weird now, etc. I hugged him, and he held me, saying Thank you! Thank you! Thank you! Thank you! Whew. People are so fragile. I have to remember that. It makes me triply nervous about this trip to San Diego. I can half-imagine pouring out a lot of love on Miguel, and half-imagine feeling trapped in hell. In which case, I leave, I guess. In either case, it's only a long weekend.

July 19: Yesterday was an intense day in Manhattan. A transformer exploded at Fortieth and Lexington, blowing a hole open in the street and disrupting midtown for a few hours. The faint but unmistakable echo of 9/11 hung in the air. I felt shaky afterward and wanted company. I called Miguel, and we talked for half an hour. He told me a story I'd sensed was coming. He had a lover who died two years ago, a loss he's only barely recovered from. A gruesome story, too. Felix was a classic daddy figure for Miguel, twelve years older. They met in Palm Springs. Miguel commuted from L.A. to San Diego for two or three years until he quit his job and moved to San Diego. Meanwhile, Felix had health problems he wasn't telling his friends about. He was diagnosed with prostate cancer and rheumatoid arthritis, and after twelve years of sobriety he started drinking heavily and alienated all of his friends in the program. He beat Miguel up so badly he landed in the hospital, and while he was out of the house Felix swallowed eighty Vicodin and two bottles of vodka. Miguel found his dead body when he got home from the hospital. Yeesh! Miguel views the death as a proud one, that Felix wanted to spare himself and Miguel the indignity of a long slow illness.

Talking to him at length made it clear how little we have in common, so this weekend together will be a little awkward. I'd like to release into letting it be loving and intimate. But I don't see us continuing afterwards. Even if we hit it off, I don't want a long-distance relationship. Maybe a "Same Time, Next Year" tryst? My fear is that he will get attached to me, and I will be the cold-hearted bitch who has to say Solly, Cholly.

July 31:

hb: Hey Miguel, I'm not in the habit of flying across the country to spend 4 days with a handsome total stranger—in fact, I've never done it before, I was surprised at how quickly you offered to host me when we first chatted online, and I was almost as surprised at how quickly I accepted. I don't know what you make of that, but the story I tell myself is that we're two guys who are hungry for an experience of sustained intimacy. We've both had intense experiences of intimacy in the past, don't have it in our lives right now, and want more of it. One thing that intimacy sort of requires is history and mutual knowledge, which we don't have. But clearly, we like each other's looks enough to give it a go.

dc: It is kinda scary for me too, handsome bud. I am NOT in the habit of inviting just anyone into my home, especially giving them the run of the place. This trip is not about "us," it is simply for your West Coast vacation. I will pick you up and drop you off at the airport, I will show you where your room is, where the towels are kept, and give you your key ... the rest will happen, if it's meant to happen. A glorified "lets meet up for a beer" type of thing.

hb: I'm not looking for a relationship right now, and I'm certainly not looking for a long-distance boyfriend. I see this as time-out-of-time, an adventure, a retreat, in all likelihood never to be repeated, but hopefully a memorable and fun occasion for all concerned.

dc: I am certainly NOT looking for a relationship right now. Given what I shared with you about Felix, it might be a while for me. Until then, I just live my life as normal. I don't go bat shit on someone if we don't click. I am not one of these insecure piano-bar queens that will give you hell if you are not attracted to me. I like playing tour guide and showing off my favorite places in San Diego, but only if you want to go there. ALSO, I am really, really, from the South: it is in my genes to be a little more trusting and hospitable. Can't help it.

hb: Maybe there will be physical chemistry, and it would be fun for that to build over time. I'd like to think there'll be some good kissing and warm cuddling. There might be some mutual cock worship. I might want to fuck you. I might want to give you a massage. But if it feels right to go the whole weekend without having sex, I'm game for that too.

dc: My main goal over the last 5 years when it comes to men is to NOT think too much about it ... no expectations. I just know what I want, and if the guy I meet is not "him" or if I am not "him" to the other guy, well, so be it! No reason to get in a fuss. Hopefully, we made friends in the process of meeting each other. 'Zat so crazy?

hb: I don't want you to have to work too hard to impress me. I am at the same time easy to get along with and difficult to satisfy—self-sufficient and independent to a fault. I look forward to hanging out with you and seeing some of your favorite places in San Diego—but please don't take offense if I'm a little boring or lazy.

dc: No offense here ... I got my life and many things to do as well. Like I said, I am here if you want some maps and direction ... or even a ride and some company. If you, for example, choose to be here and read a book for 3 days, then I would not take offense, it is your vacation, not mine.

hb: We both seem to have a streak of the romantic and a big

stripe of the realistic, and that seems like a good combo for me.

dc: YUP! You are a very attractive man, I like our communication so far, and the rest will happen "once we sniff each other like dogs."

Later that night I dream that I gave Woody Allen his first anal massage. He's sick, perhaps from cancer, wanting to experience everything before he dies. We talk about different experiences he's curious to try. He jerks himself off while I play with his butt. He's still somewhat dressed. Sad, not attractive, small thin dick.

I'm inspired NOT to hold back with Miguel this weekend. What am I saving my love (and jizz) for? Burn it up! I'll be dead soon enough.

Thursday, August 2: On the plane to San Diego, officially on vacation. It's already having the intended effect of getting me out of my tiny life and forcing me to notice new details. On the hair-raising ride to JFK, the taxi stalled in the Midtown Tunnel, so the African driver had to turn off the a/c, not sure if he'd make it. At curbside check-in, the American Airlines attendant asked, "Has anyone ever told you, you look like Elisha Cook?" The attendant was a black man in his sixties, who fondly remembered the actor from old movies such as *The Maltese Falcon* and *The Big Sleep*. On board I find myself sitting next to a young Italian couple. Across the aisle is a family of French Jews, half of whom flew in from Switzerland and made it just in time. The bald, well-spoken gay flight attendant brought an extra Budweiser, gratis, to the paterfamilias. Jew-bonding? Elder respect?

Friday, August 3: When I arrived last night, Miguel met me in his pickup truck. He took me to his bungalow in Hillcrest and showed me around a little. He put me in the guest bedroom, with a big comfortable captain's bed, as opposed to the den-like room where he sleeps in a single bed next to a flat-screen TV connected to a

PlayStation. He has the kind of living room that doesn't look very lived in; he seems to spend a lot time at his home office in a curtained alcove just off the kitchen, dominated by a gigantic monitor. We dropped my bags and walked up to University Avenue for crappy Thai food, thus beginning what I see now as an alarming pattern. He tossed out some alternatives—sushi, Mexican? I registered my preference for sushi, yet somehow we ended up at A Taste of Thai because he wanted to go there and I wanted to be agreeable. He was sexy and fiery in person, smaller and more compact than I'd pictured, but there was attraction. We kissed a little before dinner. Afterward, we went to bed. I'd said on the phone I'd like for us *not* to have sex the first night, so we could get to know each other. But he was so eager to get naked and roll around, and I was too, so I thought it would be a good warm-up. There wouldn't be fucking or cumming till later. But he turned out to be a diehard cocksucker and super-avid cum eater. He let me know that he was "thirsty," and nothing would do but for me to let him suck me off. Override of my preferences #2. Okay, fine, felt good. He had a big fat dick and a small boney butt. He definitely preferred stroking himself and sucking me to anything else. We didn't sleep together. In the morning he hijacked me in the kitchen and sucked my dick some more. We romped in bed for a while. I held off on cumming but he jerked himself off. We ate some cereal and went to Black's Beach.

Override #3: he was eager to show me Cuyamaca Falls, his favorite outdoor place, and I wanted to go. When it came to deciding where to go today, first I said Black's, then I thought, no, let me see Cuyamaca, maybe I'll fall in love with it and want to go there every day. But noooo, he decided that Black's would be too crowded on the weekend so we should go today. Fine. But then he got really sunburned on the beach. He's the local boy, I assumed he'd have his sunscreen regimen down pat. But nooo. He sucked me off again when we got home from the beach. We went out to Ichiban for sushi, then watched *Fabulous* on DVD.

Saturday, August 4: After being totally into me yesterday, suddenly this morning he was quiet and distant and unaffectionate. I took him out for breakfast. Because of his sunburn, he slept poorly and announced that he didn't want to be in the sun at all. Since we clearly weren't doing Cuyamaca, I took the truck and went back to Black's Beach by myself. He was supposedly going to nap but ended up going to Balboa Park and watching his friend Scott play volleyball. When I stopped at Peet's in Hillcrest for tea on my way back from the beach, there they were having coffee. Miguel started talking about going to Cuyamaca on Monday. I wondered if Sunday were possible. He said yes.

Sunday, August 5: This morning things became downright chilly. Despite my overt invitations to cuddle, he avoided me physically. And when I asked about the day, he said he'd like to go to the Renaissance Faire with Scott. I'd rather have poked knitting needles into my eyes. What happened to Cuyamaca? I was so upset and confused that I went for a walk while he was at his giant screen doing email. I felt abandoned, neglected, punished for some unknown infraction. I went back to his place, finally ready to ask for some clearing emotionally—but he was gone, no message. I phoned him to see where he was. He went to the store, back soon.

Being there alone, I got a chance to really take in Miguel's living environment. Considering that we were in sunny southern California, the place was surprisingly dark and cave-like. The windows were small and covered with curtains or blinds. There were no views onto the street or the neighbors' yards or the wide open sky. Maybe the layout was made for maximum privacy, since it was in a semi-suburban row of houses close together. But there was something insular and kind of creepy about it. Perfect for a vampire, or a lost weekend, or a suicidal bender.

When Miguel got back, I asked him where we stood. He finally blurted out a string of resentments and told me all the things I'd done wrong. He insisted that he wasn't mad at me, but he sounded angry and refused to make eye contact until he finally blazed at me, "You're passive-aggressive!" I almost laughed out loud at his hilarious projection.

Apparently he'd been insulted by our phone call last Sunday and my subsequent email outlining my hopes and fears for our visit. He kept saying, "You made yourself perfectly clear." I have no idea what he thought was perfectly clear, but he found it insulting and offensive and didn't say anything to me. I was just trying to put out fires at this point; clearing up misunderstandings seemed impossible. He wouldn't listen to me or take in what I said. I realized I was talking to a very insecure, paranoid individual. He was most offended, I guess, that I'd turned up my nose at his offer to show me the zoo and other tourist sites of San Diego, which he'd apparently done many times for grateful out-of-town guests. I'm sure there's a big Southern piece in there, some protocol I was supposed to follow that I wasn't aware of.

After this big blowout, in which he confirmed that he had zero sexual interest in me anymore, I felt hurt and upset. This was the nightmare I'd anticipated, being in some hostile stranger's home with a day and a half to go before my flight home. I went to my room and cried a little bit. Then I decided to pull it together and go back to the beach. He was okay with me taking the truck out again. I stopped for brunch at the Crest Café, but I was so upset I could barely eat. I called Dwight, another guy in San Diego I knew slightly, hoping he might be able to put me up for the night and take me to the airport, or at the very least have dinner with me Sunday night. But I got his voicemail. I guess I could have checked into a hotel, but the situation didn't seem that dire. Plus, I'm a cheapskate. If the only thing I'm getting out of this adventure is a free place to stay, I might as well make the most of it.

As I sat in Crest Café—my kind of yuppie diner, unlike the gross greasy spoon that Miguel preferred for breakfast—I sat next to a table of two gay male couples my age having normal conversations, and I realized how truly dysfunctional my conversations with

Miguel had been—terse, macho, devoid of ideas. It was like talking to my father or my brother-in-law. I did go back to the beach, where the weather was glorious all three days. I got some color and read André Aciman's fascinating memoir *Out of Egypt*.

Monday, August 6: Whew! In the airport at San Diego, at the close of my weekend with Miguel, which makes me seriously question my judgment. What was I thinking? I've got to stick to more solid ways of approaching contact with people I don't know. Some day, even soon, I will look back on this and it will all seem funny. But for the moment I feel shaky and emotional.

Miguel was home when I got back from the beach Sunday night. I invited him to join me for dinner, but he'd already eaten. I thought I'd check out the local leather/Levi bar, Pecs. He said Sunday was a good night to go. I invited him to join me. He said no thanks. I went to dinner at Café Eleven, where I'd eaten years ago. Now it's a sad, crappy, stuffy place for *alter kockers*. I walked to Pecs, feeling pretty good in my Diesel jeans and Butt T-shirt. I got a fair amount of attention, but the crowd seemed ugly, drunk, stupid, and desperate. I drank a beer and was ready to leave when I spotted a big tall beanpole playing pool and dancing in a sexy way when it wasn't his turn. I can't remember whether it was before or after I ordered another Sierra Nevada draft that I was surprised to get a text message from Miguel.

Wassup?

I wrote back: Watching a lanky redhead win at pool, what up w u?

He wrote back: Wondering if u were busy or wanted company. I could come to Pecs if you are gonna be there.

So—he's feeling lonely, changed his mind …?

I wrote back: Wd love company, yr place or mine?

Him: I'll be there in 20 mins.

Me: Any chance we might kiss & make up?

No reply. So I gave up hope on that mission. He eventually wrote back: No issues here, gotta stop at the ATM, be there shortly.

I walked back into the patio, keeping an eye on the sexy redhead, when someone asked me, "Are you from New York?" I said, "Yes, how can you tell?" He said, "Is your name Don?" Freaky. "Do I know you?" He turned out to be Miguel's friend Mark, there with his cute boyfriend, Greg, whom I'd just been idly cruising. Greg's mother is dying of pancreatic cancer, and he'd spent most of his time at her deathbed in the last month. We chatted. They were fun. Miguel showed up, in high spirits (drunk, I guess). We hung out for a while. I had a third beer. Then Miguel was ready to leave, so I left with him. We took a taxi back to his place. He said something about wanting to shoot some zombies, meaning play Xbox. He was being a little more friendly, so I got half-naked and lit candles in my room, on the chance that I might lure him in for last-night sex. He caught on and announced that he had no interest in having sex with me, and then he started to defend himself as if I'd accused him of leading me on. I said, "Miguel, I heard you the first time." I went back to my room and my book. He came to the door in a little while and said he didn't mean to hurt my feelings but blah blah blah. I wasn't interested in hearing him repeatedly say, "I don't want to have sex with you." I did go to watch him play Xbox in his room for a little while. He invited me to play with him, but I couldn't tolerate this cretinous activity for more than ten minutes, so I retired.

I didn't sleep well. Dropped off, then lay awake for three hours, eventually slept soundly. When I woke up, he was out. I meditated, which really helped. When he came back, I was sitting on the back porch, reading. He said a curt "Good morning," and that was it. We tiptoed around each other for a while. Next thing I knew, he'd gone into his bedroom and closed the door. No conversation about the day's schedule. I was trying to summon the open-heartedness to say, "Are you sure I can't talk you into going to Mission Beach and riding the roller coaster with me?" At the very least I wanted to ask to see a picture of Felix. But: door closed.

Luckily, Dwight called and left a message. So I showered, shaved, packed, then walked to the corner and called Dwight and asked him to come rescue me. We hung out at his house for an hour, and then he took me to the airport.

It felt creepy leaving Miguel's without saying goodbye. Sneaking out. But I couldn't see how our parting would be anything other than uncomfortable.

I left him a note on the counter that said, "I can't tell you how much I appreciate your generosity and hospitality during my stay. Best wishes, Don."

I guess, looking back at that note, maybe I am passive-aggressive.

Three Lovers

Jameson Currier

It took Richard six weeks to say he didn't love me. We were spending an afternoon in Central Park, sitting on a sheet I had taken from my apartment and unfolded on the lawn of Sheep Meadow. I was telling Richard how I wanted to see more of him, get to know him better, and that maybe we could make some trips together or take a share in a summer house in the Hamptons or the Pines. Richard answered by saying that things could go no further between us because he was getting back with his ex-lover Donnie. Richard and Donnie had been a couple for three years and ex-lovers three weeks before I met Richard at a bar on the east side of town. "It has nothing to do with you," Richard said after he told me he was breaking things off between us. Of course, it felt like it had everything to do with me. I felt like a failure because I had not convinced Richard that I could be a better lover for him than Donnie was.

It took Richard another three weeks before he actually broke things off between us. "I don't know how I can give this up," he said the afternoon we walked back to my apartment from the park and had discarded our clothes and fallen into bed again. Richard was forty-one years old and going through more crises than just breaking up and getting back with Donnie or staying with me. He had been laid off from his job as a stock analyst for a Wall Street firm, and his idleness, or lack of motivation to find a new job, was what had provoked the trouble with Donnie. Richard was not enjoying his forties; a series of root canals had left him cashless and feeling vulnerable, and the night I had met him he had complained of his brown hair graying too quickly, even though I told him it was one of his more distinctive and handsome features. I was twenty-seven years old that year and tried to prove that, together, Richard and I were ageless in bed. Richard was short and thickly built, looking more like a truck driver than a business executive, and he had a cock like a serpent, long and slender with a slightly wider head. I let him stay deep inside my body for what felt like hours; he loved it when I straddled his furry thighs so he could bury his face against my chest, whispering, "Yes, keep me here, right here, don't let me out." I was of the age that I believed that if I was passionate and involving in bed with Richard, he would be passionate and involving with me out of bed, a mistake I would make many more times with many other men.

Richard did his best to prove that it was not the quality of sex that provoked our demise. In fact, he said it was the reason why he had such trouble letting go and returning to Donnie. I did my best to show my pride was not wounded or to admit that I was again a failure as lover material by recommending Richard to a friend of a friend, a headhunter I had once dated and who specialized in finding displaced executives Wall Street positions.

Richard never thanked me for recommending him to Joel, my headhunter acquaintance, which, in turn, I also got over. Sometime later, maybe about nine or ten months, I ran into Joel in the lobby of an off-Broadway theater with our mutual friend Evan, both of whom knew of my woes with Richard. Joel mentioned that Richard had found a job at one of the city's larger banking corporations and had finally broken up with Donnie. Joel even confessed that he and Richard had gone out on a date but that there hadn't been much chemistry between them. Then Joel told me that Richard had a new boyfriend and they were part of a house Joel was putting together for the summer in East Hampton.

"I suppose you're not interested in doing a share?" Joel asked me and explained he was still trying to find someone for the final share.

"I don't think so," I answered in my most bitter and campy inflection. In the lobby of the theater, I was left with the hope that perhaps my timing or luck or both had just been out of sync with Richard, and had nothing to do with someone not wanting to know more of me outside the bedroom. Before I left to take my seat inside the theater, I asked Joel if he could recommend me as a boyfriend to any other executives who might pass his way. "Someone like Richard," I said, "but without the extra baggage."

It was a few years later when I met Mike on a phone line. Our conversation was brief, revealing our ages, height, weight, genital size, and sexual preferences in bed in the most minimal of ways. Instinct usually rules in these encounters, and I had a good feeling that I would not have to be the kind of specific sexual acrobat with Mike that other men on the phone lines so often desired. The only unsettling thing that had transpired before Mike gave me the address to his Chelsea apartment was his asking me, "Are you cute?"

I think I'm cute, and I also think I'm cuter than some of the trolls that I've met online who call themselves "hot," "handsome," or "sexy," so I answered Mike's question with my too-slick, too-practiced response, "You won't be disappointed," which I always hated having to use. Mike took my response in stride—we were, after all, hooking up to have sex, not make a porno flick, and it was a rainy, chilly Tuesday night, a time when even the hottest, most handsome, and desperately horny men seldom set out to travel, preferring instead their tricks come to them.

Mike met me at the door of his apartment, having already scrutinized me through his doorman's video camera. His apartment was tastefully decorated—solid colors, beige furniture, modern art on the walls—and he had lit candles on the coffee table as a centerpiece. He offered me a drink, which I accepted, and we talked while a hidden stereo system hummed out the notes of a jazz pianist.

Mike was close to his description of himself; his short, blond hair was thin and balding, but since he was clean shaven and wore wire-rimmed eyeglasses, he looked as academic as his perfect pronunciation suggested. In fact, in our short conversation, he admitted he taught an urban studies class at one of the downtown universities but worked full-time as an architect for a midtown firm.

On the couch, we kissed for a few minutes, and when Mike felt comfortable, he led me into a bedroom where there were more candles lit—on the nightstands, dresser top, and windowsill. Rain pelted at the window and the stereo had drifted into a sequence of softer lullabies. The overly romantic scenario and the alcohol had finally relaxed me—I'm usually very suspicious as these encounters begin—and we lay on the bed continuing our kissing, slowly undressing each other in a randomly aggressive and passionate way.

It was when we were undressed and I was lying on top of Mike that I got an eerie sensation that Mike's attention had been pulled out of the room. Looking over my shoulder, I saw the shadow of a man standing at the door. My body tensed from fear, and a startled sweat broke out at my forehead, armpits, and back. I had not known that there was someone else in the apartment—Mike had not indicated that he shared the space and I had not heard anyone come in, and I had not detected Mike speaking to anyone when he had gone out of the living room and gotten us drinks. I rolled off of Mike and swung my feet over the side of the bed and reached for my T-shirt and underwear on the floor, defensive enough to throw a punch if that was what the scenario required. My heart was beating heavily in my ears, but somehow I heard Mike say, "Happy Birthday, darling."

The man in the doorway moved further into the room and Mike reached out to me and said, "Don't go."

"What's going on?" I asked. I was worried that the man might be angered—I still had not seen his face and he stood at the doorway with his hands crossed against his chest.

"Looks like my gift is as surprised as I am," the man said. The tone of his voice, the same calm, practiced sort of speech as Mike's, was layered with a brilliant glee and made me stop getting dressed, though my heart continued crashing inside my chest.

"You don't think I was going to get you a hustler?" Mike said.

"You could have done that on your own."

"So instead, you've hustled our new friend, who seems not to know anything about me."

The man was now closer in the room and I could see he was startlingly handsome—dark, slick-backed hair, dark eyes, with a slender European style about him. I immediately understood why Mike took whatever steps he could to please this sort of man, even to the expense of luring a stranger into bed. The man radiated sex, and it seemed to me that he was the kind of man it was not easy to possess because life could offer him potential distractions it would not necessarily offer others.

Mike introduced me to Tino, his lover for two years. Tino was turning forty the following day, or rather, at the stroke of midnight, only a few minutes away. Tino and Mike settled my nerves and Mike fetched more drinks—a bottle of champagne was opened and poured into long, thin glasses. We talked a bit more in the bedroom—mostly my lobbing questions at Tino to dispel my anxieties, until Mike toasted Tino at midnight. Tino responded with a kiss—first for Mike and then with me, and then he drew us easily into a lovely and unexpected threesome.

That was not my first or last three-way, and I must confess that Mike and Tino paid more attention to me than they did to each other, as if I were the one celebrating a birthday. I've not done enough of these threesome encounters, however, to be an expert on their psychological construction. But it was clear to me even on that night that there was an imbalance in their relationship. It was a few years later when I think I finally understood what Mike had been trying to do that night we hooked up on the phone. By then I was in my forties and in my first relationship with a man to last more than six months, and I was looking for ways I could justify keeping our unbalanced relationship going. Keith was also in his early forties, recently divorced from his wife and out on his own for the first time as a newly minted openly gay man. His years as a suburban high school math teacher had given him a conceited arrogance, and he now found everything about gay life as sexually exciting as would a teenager just discovering the power of his dick. Among his newly articulated fantasies was his desire for a "hot three-way," something that though I did not discourage him from finding, I did not want to participate in with him myself. Keith had a stinginess to his personality which I had grown to dislike the more I knew him better—a sort of this-is-what-I-deserve-because-I-have-been-in-the-closet-for-such-a-long-time—that I knew whatever three-way encounter we could have would leave me as the odd partner out. I could clearly imagine him luring another man into bed in the same way Mike had lured me, yet Keith would never have been as accommodating in the way Tino had. Keith, in fact, would have made me watch him make love to someone else, as if it were a way to punish me for the bad behavior of revealing my insecurities over our relationship. I was wildly attracted to Keith, more so than he was to me, which had set up our inequality since our first date. Keith was the sort of man who wanted a boyfriend who wouldn't mind him having other boyfriends, and though I tried my best to be that sort of man, it just wasn't where I was headed at that moment.

Keith had also complicated our relationship by leaving clues of his other sexual involvements—Post-It Notes with names and addresses seemed to float out of garbage pails or wave at me from desk drawers to catch my attention; phone messages would begin on his answering machine while we were in bed having sex, "Uh, Keith, this is Joe, we met last week ..."

I suppose I should have just abandoned Keith, given him up, but psychologically I couldn't admit another defeat. I had come this far. I thought if I found a way not to care about Keith's other activities, I could find a way for our relationship to work for me, and I pursued several options—meditation and yoga, long hours at the gym, easing my confusion with a series of strong drinks—none of which worked. I also considered ways in which I might be more sex-positive; I thought about suggesting we go to a sex club together or participate in a three-way, though I could not commit myself to actually discussing these possibilities with Keith. Which was how I found my way into a bar in the East Village one night and where, slightly inebriated and finally relaxed, I met Jesse.

Jesse was in his late twenties and perhaps the tallest of all my lovers, 6' 4", long-legged, hairless, and lean, with the pale, chiseled physique of a swimmer. He was a corporate lawyer who spoke in such a soft, dull monotone that I would have to blink to maintain my attention. Jesse was much more lively in bed, however, and he made me feel like a young man myself with his slender legs propped up against my shoulders and his ass willing to accept my cock. It was the fifth or sixth time with Jesse when things turned sour—impotence struck me for the first time in bed with a man. I knew I should have been moving into a deeper emotional involvement with Jesse, but I couldn't because I still had Keith lodged deeply in my consciousness. I knew I couldn't go any further with Jesse unless I confessed the truth about myself because I had been dishonest with him from the start—never mentioning that there was another man. It was as if Keith were already in bed with us, commenting on Jesse's attributes, ready to take him for himself.

Jesse didn't seem to mind my inability to perform—he was firmly erect, and I could have gone ahead and been the evening's passive partner. But my frustration was caught in my throat and I began a short crying jag that startled both of us. Jesse held me the way a concerned lover would—exactly the kind of lover I always wanted—and I unraveled the whole misery of my affair with Keith, and for the first time I understood what Richard must have been feeling the afternoon he had told me we could go no further.

When I had finished my tale and restored my emotional stability, Jesse said, "I've not been honest myself." It was now my turn to embrace him as he confessed his ongoing relationship with a guy who lived out of town, his former college boyfriend. Together, Jesse said, they were great in bed, but neither of them would commit to giving up their lives and careers away from each other, so they only saw each other once a month on visits. The moment Jesse began talking about his boyfriend, Chip, the better I felt, as if I knew that I no longer had to be a major player for Jesse, or he for me.

Although our sexual chemistry had failed to ignite that night after our confessions, it was not my last encounter with Jesse. I did not give up on Keith right away, either; I found myself in deeper despair before I found my path out. But there was an evening when Keith and I went as boyfriends to a gallery opening in Tribeca, and we ran into Jesse, who was friends with one of the artists in the exhibit. As I introduced one lover to the other, I sensed Keith's interest in Jesse as a potential and younger sexual partner and Jesse's interest in Keith because he had witnessed my tale of woe over this man. I sensed that I could have possibly engineered a three-way that night, but I didn't attempt it. Instead, I walked away from both of them and their growing conversation, hoping they might hit it off together on their own, without me. They didn't, of course, and I was spared the humiliation of watching one's lovers walk off into the sunset together, arm in arm. But it was a defining moment. Watching them from the other side of the gallery with a drink in my hand, I finally understood I was on my way to someone else.

The Telephone Line

Jerry L. Wheeler

Fantasies take you into dangerous territory, especially those with a chance of coming true. One false move, one wrong smell, one slight imperfection, and the whole thing comes crashing down. Nothing—from the idea to the execution—can bear any weight again, and it can't possibly be reconstructed. Nope. Fantasies are nothing to play with.

So, when one does threaten to become reality, don't fuck with it. Let it flow naturally. Don't try to hurry it along or do anything differently than you've had in your head the last forty or fifty times you played it. Know your lines, work your blocking, come in on cue, and it'll materialize right before your eyes. That's what happened to me.

I had just gotten my first computer—back when only dial-up was available—and I soon tired of missing phone calls from friends and family because I was online having "fun," which meant trolling the few gay chat rooms available, looking for phone sex. I called Qwest, the local phone company, to arrange for a second line. A few days later, the technician showed up.

His name was Clint or Curt or Chet or something. I can only vaguely recall letters embroidered in a white oval patch on his uniform shirt. His shoulder-length hair was dirty blond and his eyes were green and reddened. Company regulations probably forbade him from smoking pot in the truck on the way to his calls, but I was relatively certain he'd had a bong hit or two for breakfast.

"Wheeler?" he asked as I opened the door to my house trailer.

He punctuated his question with a slight toss of his head to get his hair out of his eyes.

I have no idea what I said. I was concentrating on not drooling. He was in his early to mid-twenties. A surfer-boy type—definitely straight and hot to death, from the stubble on his face and neck to the way the frayed cuffs of his JC Penney's Levi knockoffs caught in the top of his scuffed tan work boots.

The repairman/phone guy/delivery man scenario has been a staple of gay (and straight) fantasies from the earliest days of eight-millimeter film loops and probably way before then. Burly men in jeans and uniform shirts, half sweaty from their labors, rumpled, wrinkled, and ready for action they're not getting from their wives or girlfriends—what's not to jerk off over?

Most of the service guys who have come to the house haven't been prime meat—I mean, some plumbers' cracks you just don't wanna see. Clint/Curt/Chet, however, was a dream on my doorstep, redolent of repair truck musk with a faint hint of a morning Lifebuoy shower. I was determined to have his dick in my mouth before the paperwork was done.

Trying to recall how much pot I had in the house, I brought him in and led him to my computer desk and the junction box where I wanted the second line installed. His jeans fit perfectly—not too tight but snug enough to accentuate the soft curve of his ass. I was glad I'd worn underwear or my sweats would have had a noticeable tent.

"Looks pretty simple," he said with the practised assurance of a professional telephonic diagnostician. Must be something they learned at the training sessions to pacify customers. His confidence was making me hornier, if that was possible. "All I gotta do is find the phone box outside, run another line inside, and bring it up though the floor. Lemme get some tools, and I'll be right back."

The next fifteen minutes were torture as I rolled a joint, paced, and wondered what to do when he came back in. Should I have a porn tape in the video? But I had no straight porn—not even bi stuff. And gay porn might scare him off. It was too early for a beer, so I'd have to try getting him stoned.

I love straight guys, single or married. I love gay men too—when it comes to dick, I'm an equal opportunity cocksucker. Some gay men might call that self-loathing, but I don't believe it. I like myself and I like being gay. However, straight guys have an enticing air of casual masculinity that many gay men just can't capture.

The difference is embodied by the popular phrase, "straight-acting." Straight guys don't have to act. It's just how they are. Of course, all men have masculinity—but too often gay men tend to bury it beneath other culturally learned traits or accentuate it to cartoonish extremes. That's why they have to "act." Just like a fantasy, masculinity vanishes when you fuck with it.

Meanwhile, Clint/Curt/Chet was back in the house and crawling underneath my desk, drilling a hole in the floor to run the second line to the junction box. His squirming and reaching had pulled the shirt out of his jeans, exposing the small of his tanned back, dusted with a faint coat of darker blond hair.

Trying to adjust my hard-on so it was less apparent, I resolved to scrutinize and respond to any hint of an opportunity. After all, I was a Qwest customer, and he was on official company business and had to conduct himself like an employee. He could hardly punch me out if he wanted to keep his job. Besides, adverse reactions and possible physical injury go with straight-guy territory. The danger's part of the allure.

Finished with his drilling, my quarry went back under the trailer and fished the line up through the floor. As he breezed through the kitchen on his way to connect it to the junction box, I stopped him.

"You want something to drink? Water? A Coke?"

"A Coke would be great, thanks," he said, flashing a lopsided grin that stayed with me even after he'd left the room.

Grabbing a can from the fridge, I popped the top and snatched the joint I'd rolled off the counter. I lit it, trailing smoke into the office as I put the Coke down on the desk and knelt down beside him. "How's it going?" I asked.

"Almost done." As soon as he got a whiff of the pot, his head came up like a pointer looking for game. I smiled and held the spliff out to him. His hand came up almost automatically and reached for the joint. Then he stopped himself. "Can't, man," he said. "I'm still on the clock. Sure smells good, though."

I let him think about it. In a few moments, the junction box was back together and he was reaching around the back of my computer. "That should do it," he said, standing back. "You wanna boot it up?"

"Yeah." I held the joint out and sat down at my desk. "Hold this for me, willya?"

This time there was no hesitation. He took a nice, long toke while Windows 95 loaded, and I was soon looking at my AOL home page. He exhaled, chugged half a can of Coke and belched. "Sorry," he said with that grin of death (it was sure killing me). He took another hit before he spoke. "Hey, can I use your bathroom real quick?"

Perfect. My opening. All I had to do was work up the nerve to say my line, which is where I usually choke. Either my brain or my tongue or my intestinal fortitude fails me, and I end up on the wrong side of Regret Street, just this side of Missed Opportunities. But not this time.

"Only if I can help," I said as casually as I knew how.

As soon as I said it, I searched his face trying to figure out which way the wind was gonna blow. I didn't have to wait long. He raised his eyebrows once, exhaled blue smoke and chuckled. *Chuckled.* "You mean, like, help me piss?"

"Yeah."

He took another puff and looked at me for a few seconds before he shrugged. "Okay," he said. "There's gotta be a first time for everything, right?" I didn't know if he was trying to convince me or himself, but I figured the question was rhetorical, so I didn't answer. I just led the way to the bathroom, my heart pounding.

When we walked in, my disheveled bathroom caused a twinge of shame, but I soon got over it. A straight guy wouldn't think a glob or two of shaving cream in the sink and a few pubes on the toilet rim was much of a mess. And when he bent over and lifted the seat, he didn't recoil in horror. In fact, he stood there smirking at me as he hit on the joint again.

"I gotta piss," he said. "I thought you wanted to help."

Nothing—I mean absolutely nothing—gets me hotter than watching guys piss. I'm not really into watersports, so it's not the end product. It's more the process. Pissing is the only time it's socially acceptable for guys to touch their dicks around other guys.

And touch them they do. They flop them out, shake them, pull on them, scratch them. They even sneak peeks at other guys' dicks to see if theirs measures up—all within the furtive, nervous parameters of urinal behavior, of course. Damn those newfangled privacy shields. Give me good old-fashioned trough pissing any day.

But never, before or since, have I had the opportunity to help a guy piss. I had meant to say watch, and it wasn't until Clint/Curt/Chet reminded me of my responsibility that I realized what he'd agreed to. And there he was, waiting patiently for me to reach inside his pants, fish out his dick, and hold it for him.

My hands trembled as I unsnapped and unzipped his jeans; edging closer to him, I felt the warmth of his body. He didn't pull away. It wasn't a joke. It was really going to happen. My tremors subsiding with this knowledge, I pushed the denim aside and slid my fingers down past the waistband of his white Hanes.

His pubes were lush and dense and his male scent floated up to my nose. I wanted to linger in that fragrant, wiry patch forever, but the poor guy had to pee. I took hold of his soft, warm dick with one hand and used the other to pull down the front of his underwear and ease his hairy nuts over the waistband.

As soon as I aimed his dick at the toilet bowl, he let go. A few drops became a little flow, then a full, strong stream. He sighed with relief as he pissed, then he took another hit and put the joint on the edge of the sink. If I'd had a third hand to touch myself with,

I would have come right then. I almost did, anyway.

All too soon he stopped. Piss dribbled on my fingers. I waggled his cock in the air, drops flying everywhere, but the unsure feeling came back. Was I just supposed to put it back now? Was it all over? I didn't want to let go of it, and Clint/Curt/Chet wasn't giving me much direction now that his bladder had been emptied. I decided to take the matter into my own hands.

So to speak.

I went from waggling his dick to caressing the head of it while I brought my other hand up to his balls and stroked them. He sighed again, leaning forward and restoring my confidence. And if that motion hadn't convinced me, his rapidly stiffening cock did. I sank to my knees and took it into my mouth, pushing him back against the sink.

Size? I can't recall, and it really isn't important anyway. I remember it was cut, but that's about all. The visuals never stick with me, but the dicksmell does. Faintly pissy but mostly musky, it's an incredibly male perfume whose base is common to all guys, with room for individual variation in its topnotes.

I don't know how long I sucked him, but we took turns driving. Sometimes he grabbed my head and fucked my mouth with rough thrusts. Other times I had my hands on his hairy ass, forcing his cock down my throat as far as I could take it. At last he began breathing heavy and his balls tensed.

He tried to pull me off, but I'd worked too hard to be denied a creamy dessert. I pinned his hands to the counter and used my weight to keep them down as he bucked against me a few times before he exploded. Spurts of hot, salty cum filled my mouth. He gasped as I swallowed. I didn't let him up until I was sure he'd been drained.

"God damn," he said. "Jesus."

I tucked his dick back in his shorts and left him to zip up. He took a few minutes to wash his hands and emerged looking hasty and sheepish. Uh-oh, I thought. Straight guilt. He didn't say anything and didn't even look my way. He took his clipboard off the kitchen table and handed it to me.

"Um … I got another call to get to. If you'll just sign down at the bottom, so they can bill ya, I'll be on my way." Then he smirked again. Maybe handling his clipboard gave him some feeling of normalcy. "I'd let ya go for nothin', but my boss'd wonder."

But I didn't mind getting charged, and—this is true—it was $69.69. A small price to pay for a fantasy.

It can happen for you too. With a little luck, some nerve, and the right timing, your straight guy fantasy can become a masturbatory memory. Just make sure you have plenty of weed and/or beer.

And leave the bathroom door open.

Magic Fingers

Paul Bellini

As a child, I had scoliosis, a curvature of the spine. Essentially, my rib cage was slightly twisted, not aligned with the rest of my body, so that my right side formed a gentle hump and the left side a gentle indentation. Although this was unnoticeable to the naked eye, I nevertheless identified with Quasimodo, not a good thing for a fat, insecure gay teenager living in a small northern mining town.

They sent me to a chiropractor. He was a handsome young man with thick glasses that made his eyes bug out. I loved his Beatles haircut, and my weekly visits to his office for realignment were a treat. I got to skip classes and receive a very physical medical treatment from the sort of man I would grow up wanting to marry. The best treatment was the one in which he would hug me with both arms, and then slam his body weight down on me, causing my spine to snap back into its proper position. I called it the Lovin' Embrace. For once, an affliction was paying off.

In my thirties, the back pain persisted. My sister suggested that I consider therapeutic massage. I soon became an addict, going from one clinic to the next, always requesting a male massage therapist "because they're stronger, and I need deep tissue work." Of course, that's bullshit. One of the strongest grips I ever felt was from a female massage therapist. Mostly, I just hoped to score a cutie.

But the day came when I realized that I wanted to be a pitcher, not just a catcher. I decided I had to give someone a back rub. There was an antecedent. When I was around seven or eight, my handsome young cousin, only a few years my senior, would pay me a quarter to rub his back. Could he possibly have known how thrilling this duty would be to me? He was long and lean, and it was the first time I got to touch another boy's body. I decided then and there to become a masseur.

In hindsight, as I struggle with my writing career, I wish I had taken that choice more seriously. I could use a sideline, especially one with such potential for arousal. My clients would call me Dr Paul, and only my receptionist would notice that my clientele consisted entirely of hot boys.

Many years later, I found a way to make this fantasy a reality—when I met Chris, an impossibly handsome sex trade worker, on Yonge Street. Chris was well over six feet tall, with what's known on hookup sites as a swimmer's build. Not that he ever swam, or did anything other than take drugs and jerk off, but that's beside the point. Chris and I hooked up outside of my apartment building. I had seen him working the streets, and I was more than interested. He was a great beauty, a stunning blond with blue eyes, dimples, and a tiny cleft in his perfectly formed chin. Every time he saw me, he'd break out a grin that lit up the skies. Pity that crack had destroyed most of his teeth.

So the deal was made. But when Chris came to my apartment, I realized that he was too tall for me. When I stood before him, my nose landed somewhere between his nipples. I wanted desperately to kiss this wrecked beauty, but that would mean I had to stand on a crate, like Alan Ladd had to do for most of his movie career. We were longitudinally incompatible. I was about to send him away when Chris, bored with my fidgeting, said that his back was sore from sleeping on concrete all night, and would I mind if he stretched out on my bed. Without waiting for an answer, he went into the bedroom and tore off his shirt, revealing a lean, ripped torso, naturally hairless and utterly delectable.

"Gonna lay down for a bit, yo," he said, groggy and wasted from a night of drugging and fucking. He hit the mattress face down. So, what do I do? I thought. Then, looking at that solid slab of muscle and skin, I had an epiphany. I was going to become the masseur that I had always dreamed of becoming.

I mounted his ass. "Don't fuck me," he mumbled into the pillow. Our jeans were still on and zipped up, and that's not where I was going, anyhow.

"Just lie there and relax," I said. "I'm going to give you the back rub of your life."

"Yeah, okay," he grunted softly. From where I sat, he looked like a young Clint Eastwood. At first slowly, I started rubbing my palms up and down the flat of his back. He groaned, clearly enjoying my gentle touch. Then, once the flesh was sufficiently warmed and pliable, I began delicately kneading it, grabbing it as one does the back of a kitten's neck.

"Oooo," he groaned. "That's fuckin' great, bro."

I continued, now digging my fingertips into the muscle around his shoulder blades. I could feel small calcium deposits, which I worked back and forth in an effort to disintegrate them. I had learned a lot from my years as a back patient. "Yeah, right there," he moaned as my magic fingers kneaded and prodded and massaged various trouble spots. The whole time, my erection sang, so happy was I to finally realize my dream. Nay, not merely a dream but a fetish.

How liberating.

I worked my way down to the small of his back, which my high school theater arts teacher had told our Grade Ten class was an erogenous zone. I rotated my thumbs along his spine. Chris writhed in ecstasy, groaned with pleasure, and broke out in goose bumps. He was mine! God, I'm good at this, I thought.

Then I worked the back of his neck and head, where so much tension resides, carefully using my fingernails to scratch his scalp. I loved running my fingers through his hair. Now, normally, massage therapists do not venture into this territory, but I was so aroused I completely forgot my professional (well, amateur) demeanor. I played with his hair, a lovely blond mop, gently stroked his face and jaw, thrilled by the texture of stubble on his cheeks. He looked so sexy at that moment I couldn't resist. I leaned down and kissed the side of his face.

"Garlic breath," he groaned, cracking his eyes open just a little to squint at me. "Is lip massage part of the deal?"

I tried to kiss him again, but he got up, pushing me off him. "Thanks for the massage, bro," he said, putting his shirt back on. I have since learned that when the hustler says it's over, it's over. I was surprised, but not very, when after the magnificent job I did, he had the nerve to ask for payment. That was when I learned that if you cook a hustler dinner, he will probably charge you for having to eat it. So I gave him seventy bucks, which is about what it would have cost me to have a massage therapist give me a treatment.

Despite my best efforts, I have never given anyone a back rub of this magnitude since. But every time my back aches, which is often, given the scoliosis, I think of Chris. By merely lying there, he gave me all I ever needed.

OK! OK! IT'S... WELL, I...

I'VE ALWAYS WANTED TO SEE BATMAN AND ROBIN FUCK. I WANT TO BE THE VILLAIN WHO MAKES THEM FUCK...

OKAAAY...

WE CAN DO THAT.

I WENT ABOUT MAKING ARRANGEMENTS. FIRST, I CALLED MY BOYFRIEND AT THE TIME KEVIN, WHO WAS ALSO A PORN STAR, AND HIRED HIM TO BE BATMAN.

THEN I ORDERED THE COSTUMES... THEY WERE RIDICULOUSLY EXPENSIVE BUT THE CLIENT WAS LOADED AND DIDN'T FLINCH AT THE ESCALATING COSTS.

WAIT, ARE YOU KIDDING?

I HAVE TO SAY THIS SHIT WITHOUT LAUGHING?

KEVIN... WE HAVE TO PLAY THIS SCENE COMPLETELY SERIOUSLY!

WOW! THESE OUTFITS ARE AMAZING!

HERE. YOU'VE GOT LINES TO MEMORIZE.

HE'S EMBARRASSED ENOUGH ABOUT THIS FANTASY... IT WOULD DEVESTATE HIM IF HE FELT LIKE WE WERE MAKING FUN OF HIM...

NOW I HAVE TO GO SHOWER AND SHAVE MY LEGS...

WHAT!?

I LOVE SUPERHEROES!

ROBIN DOES **NOT** HAVE HAIRY THIGHS, AS MUCH AS YOU LIKE THEM...

WELL, IF I WAS A SUPERHERO, I'D HAVE MY SIDEKICK RUNNING AROUND IN CHAPS WITH HIS HAIRY ASS HANGING OUT...

WHICH IS WHY YOU SHOULD STICK TO PORN.

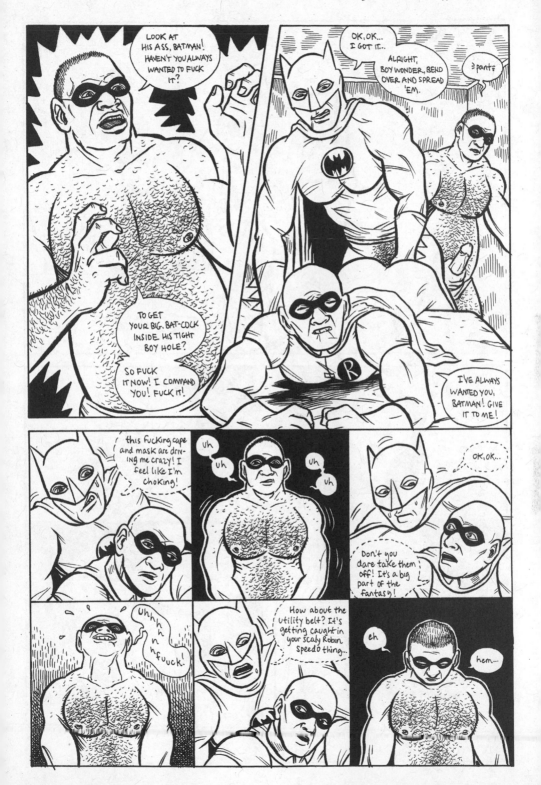

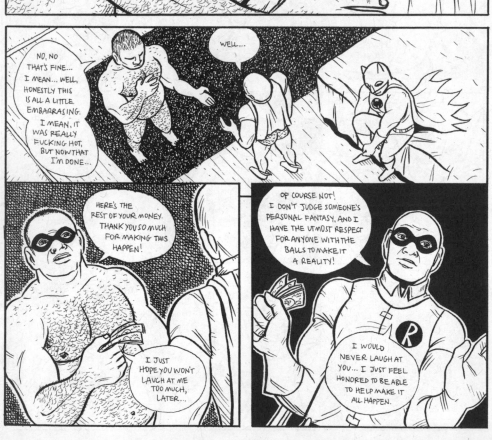

The Truth of His Nakedness

Lewis DeSimone

There are no rules. I can't tell you precisely what draws me to a man, can't predict what look or gesture or body part will bring that special lightness to my belly, that feathery tickle to my throat. When I try to explain, the words crumble like dried paint, and I am left with only images—flashes of insight, apparitions of lust transfigured into something larger, something beyond understanding. The erotic makes everything clear, if only for a moment—transcendently clear. And then the moment is gone.

The erotic is Monet in reverse: It makes sense only up close. From a distance, it's all a blur.

My lover reclines across the length of the hot tub, buoyed above me by the warm, gentle water. I trace a line from his neck down over the slope of his chest. Myriad dark hairs curl over his nipple like the tentacles of an anemone. I swirl my finger around and around, pushing the hairs gently away, lifting the nipple awake.

We spent most of the morning in bed, alternately sleeping and making love, the one flowing effortlessly into the other, as though the sex were akin to REM sleep, just another stage in an endless cycle. Emerging from a dream, I turned over in bed and rested my head on his bare shoulder, uncurled my fingers softly against his chest. With him beside me, holding me in his nakedness, I had no reason to get up.

Even now, after dragging ourselves downstairs to breakfast, we heed the call of the hot tub out back—another chance to be naked together, this time surrounded by the trees that line the yard, our flesh exposed to the sky. As his body floats above mine, feet pressed against the far wall of the tub, strong legs suspended in the water, I can't take my eyes off his pink skin, the fullness of him, the truth of his nakedness.

I can be turned on by a look, a caress, even the right word. But that's only what gets things started, the initial tug that draws me to pull his clothes off, to lift my arms into the air so he can remove my shirt, to hold my legs together so he can pull off my pants. In the end, it's all about being naked.

For me, the most erotic thing is the shape of a man's torso—the way the pectoral muscles carve out a hard ridge above the belly, the way the belly itself curves out just a bit (not too little, not too much) before tapering down to the crotch. Cover it all in a soft coat of fur, and I'm a goner.

There's a vulnerability to the belly. That's probably why I've never been too fond of overly defined abdominal muscles. Abs protect the belly; they hold it in the way ribs defend the chest. To me, nakedness is about vulnerability, exposure, rawness. "The thing itself; unaccommodated man," as King Lear said when he saw the naked Edgar dancing madly on the heath.

We hide behind our clothes—the shirt that brings out the blue in our eyes, the jacket that's trimmed to disguise the paunch. We put on power suits to project an image of control—to give us a confidence we might not feel without that magic necktie. We relish the strong click of our boot heels against the pavement, the way the right pair of glasses frames the face. Clothes make the man, they say. But all they really do is make the image of a man: clothes cover up the truth of who a man is.

When I am naked with someone, it's about more than the shape of his legs or the texture of the hair at the back of his neck or the size of his cock. When I am naked with a man, we are both exposed—that's the whole point. I can't hide when I'm naked, and neither can he.

You know your relationship is in trouble when he starts wearing pajamas to bed.

Nakedness used to scare me. In junior high, when we would play basketball in gym class, I would pray to be chosen for the "shirts" team and not the "skins." Fully clothed or not, I was a hopeless athlete, of course, which was reason enough for the merciless taunts. To be physically exposed, as well, was still more threatening—as if the other boys could see not just my skin, but beneath it, as if the exposure of my skin could reveal my desire for theirs.

I could be comfortably naked only in the privacy of my bedroom. A couple of years earlier, on the brink of puberty, I would often retreat to my room after dinner and simply lie naked on my bed, watching TV by myself. In those innocent days, I relished nudity— even before I knew what to do with the hard-on that inevitably appeared once I'd stripped off my clothes.

I didn't have language for it at the time, but those youthful moments of nakedness were my first real experience of the erotic. Even without touching myself—not even running a finger down my leg or planting a soft kiss on my forearm—I was creating a space for sensuality. I knew enough to keep a watchful ear for a knock at the door. I knew enough to have my pajamas at the ready, so I could claim to have been in the middle of changing. But I was too young to feel shame on those evenings. My nakedness wasn't about sex; it was about being natural. There was an energy to it that I couldn't define then: those few moments were my island of time, in an otherwise other-focused day, to be wholly myself.

It wasn't about sex. Until it was. But it took me years to realize that nothing had really changed. These days, my nakedness is usually reserved for sexual situations, but that only reinforces the point—the erotic space is the same. The erotic space is the space of unavoidable truth. The erotic space is who I am.

The conventional desire is to be loved for who you are, not for who people think you are—the image they project of you, the way you remind them of an old relationship (a lover, a parent) they long to heal. You want to be loved for who you actually are, for your talents and interests, your hopes and dreams. But, in the end, are we any better at defining ourselves than anyone else is? When all is said and done, even those things we believe most strongly—the aspects of character to which the ego holds fast—are just window dressing. In the end, all there is is the nakedness: two bodies coming together, sharing their common humanity, their naked vulnerability, the ultimate truth that we are not alone.

Several years ago I had a lovely date with a man I knew I'd never see again. He was moving to Portland the following week, on the verge of a new life that would not involve the man he'd just met, no matter how strong our initial attraction. I remember being taken by his soul patch—that little square of hair beneath his lower lip, his homage to a beard. I remember the blue of his eyes, the glasses he took off when we kissed. And I remember making love to him in my bed, in my cozy San Francisco apartment. He was a playful lover, and at one point—knowing this was our only chance to be together—he asked if I had any fantasies I'd like to fulfill. I thought for a moment, looking into his eyes, my hands caressing his sturdy, broad shoulders.

"Yes," I replied at last. "Let's pretend we've never done this before. Let's pretend it's our first time."

And that night it was. That night, I was a virgin, exploring another man's body for the first time—the firmness of the hips, the softness under his arm that made him squirm at my touch. That night I held him tenderly, this total stranger I would never see again, and I relived the romance of novelty, the way my heart had felt years before, the real first time I'd ever touched another man.

In our fantasy, we returned to a place of innocence where our histories didn't matter, where there was no history—only two bodies coming together. That night, we could pretend we were in love, because there was no danger we'd have to put it to the test in the morning.

We didn't know each other, of course, but that didn't prevent something magical from happening. It didn't keep the evening from becoming a memory that still lives within me. Over dinner, he may have told me about himself—where he grew up, what he did for a living, what he'd studied in school—but I don't remember any of that. All I remember is the way he looked, the way his body felt against mine, and the certainty that that was enough.

I didn't know his name. I never knew their names—the silent men lurking in the corners, passing me on the stairs with a sultry backward glance, reaching a hand out to pull me into the darkness. I had no idea who he was outside this room with its dim light and the steady footfalls of other strangers pacing around, searching for someone to be with for a time. Our connection was triggered by a look held a beat too long, and a finger boldly brushing against a nipple. That was enough.

We found a space of our own, as private as a space could be in a room built for voyeurs and exhibitionists. And we came together wordlessly, signaling our desires through other means. His body told me what to do. His body was more eloquent than most men's words. And in that moment, in that space, I knew him. There were no mysteries because there were no questions, no expectations. He was. I was. We were.

I can count on one hand the truly transcendent experiences of my life—those moments when I felt connected to the energy of the world in an unmistakable, heart-in-your-stomach, yet oddly peaceful way. Once, when my infant nephew fell asleep on my chest. Again when, as a hospice volunteer, I held the hand of a man I hardly knew and watched him die. And again, in a darkened bedroom with a quiet man I loved, but only for a time.

After months together, we had settled into a sexual routine: he would come home from work and find me in bed, and we would go through the motions—he moved this way, I moved that way, and eventually we both came. We had gotten it down to a science.

But once—just once—science gave way to art, or something even greater. In the middle of it—the two of us wrapped in an embrace, our arms wound tightly around each other—I had the distinct sensation of floating in space. I imagined us cradled together in a cocoon of some sort, hovering in the blackness of the universe—beyond gravity, beyond place and time. We were weightless, suspended in the unseen, protective arms of the universe.

And then we weren't.

Absence has its own role to play in my erotic history. How many lovers are invested with special powers simply because they refuse to be possessed? The first, the one who never fully gave himself to me—because he couldn't, or he wouldn't—is, ironically, the one who holds the greatest sway. I eroticized his unavailability, making too much of the rare moments we shared, the moments I lived for, for years. In memory, he still creeps up behind me at the stove and wraps his arms around my waist as I stir the Bolognese. In memory, his mustache still tickles my lip as we kiss.

And when he leaves, each time he leaves, the touch of his hand remains on my skin. His smell lingers in the sheets, and I tip my nose into the pillow to recapture a piece of him—the sweat of his armpits, the musk of his crotch. I hear his voice whispering in my ear—*yes, baby, that's it, baby*—an endless loop, as if the very words are trapped inside, running in circles, waiting for his return to complete them.

I miss him already—instantly, as soon as the door closes behind him and the room seems to grow that much smaller. I pace the floor for an eternity of minutes before finally stopping by the table, where his wine glass still sits, the print of his lips still smeared on the rim. That's when my knees fold up and my body sinks beneath me like a rickety boat that has, at last, taken on too much water. I slip to the floor—the hard, uneven floor that stabs my feet with splinters, stigmata of love. I slip to the floor, and the tide of tears breaks over me.

I see his chest—pinkish brown areolas the size of sand dollars, surrounded by hair in a butterfly pattern, like mine. I see every inch of him, still—alone in that room, in my youthful pain, in the belief that I would never love like that again, that I had no choice but to accept the pain, a pain that, though it threatened to crush my lungs like an anchor, was better than the emptiness without it. I see every inch of him, still, across miles and years that have brought more love, more pain, more hope and disappointment. I see first love in all its drama, all its absurdity. And I know that, for good or ill, it's true: I never have loved that way again.

Bathhouse of Desires

Jay Starre

I was nervous. The entrance in the darkened downtown Vancouver street was marked only by a number, with no welcoming neon sign broadcasting Gay Sex Here!

I'd seen an ad for the place in the classifieds, under the personals. Though my hopes were high, I wasn't expecting much—certainly not what I found, a steamy miasma of desires rampant and desires fulfilled.

It was 1980. I was twenty-five, divorced, and living in the interior of British Columbia on an isolated ranch. My neighbors were a mix of hippie back-to-the-land dropouts and staid country folk who'd farmed the rural valleys for generations.

I was horny—very horny. Desperately horny. I needed to be touched by another man, by almost any other man, and in almost any way.

Inside the doorway, I found a small entrance hall, a locked door to the right, and a glassed-in booth to the left with a hole for the attendant to speak through. My heart pounded and my hands trembled—from desire, from nerves, and from an ingrained fear of being caught.

Caught being gay.

Even years later, whenever I entered a bathhouse, that same mix of emotions gripped me, the same pounding heart, the same trembling hands.

A small sign above the booth proclaimed Hornby Steam. A smaller sign offered proof I was where I wanted to be: This is a gay establishment.

The guy behind the glass was easy-going, explaining how much a locker or a room would cost, how many hours I had, and, finally, where my room would be, beyond that locked door to my right.

I was a country boy. I looked him in the eye, though I was nervous, and he smiled. Behind him, above the bank of room lockboxes, I saw a row of sex toys for sale, on bold display. Dildos I couldn't imagine fitting up my tight ass, or any ass for that matter, of all colors and shapes.

This was the place I was looking for.

A buzzer sounded. I pushed open the heavy door to my right. I was inside.

Dimly lit, with throbbing disco music blaring, the bathhouse was vaguely reminiscent of the gay nightclubs I'd previously sought out. A small change area, with lockers for those who chose the cheaper route, was to my right, a darkened corridor to my left. I couldn't believe how much I was shaking. Anticipation of sex!

A trio of men was changing; two sent furtive glances my way, and one stared boldly. I looked away, afraid to meet their eyes, afraid to acknowledge why I was there.

In search of room eighty-one, I took two paces into the dimly lit hallway before I was struck by the reality of my situation.

A doorway into one of the cubicles was ajar. I slowed and peered in.

A heat wave of near-paralyzing lust shocked me. A man was sprawled on a narrow bed. On his stomach. Naked. Entirely naked. Legs spread. Bared ass a sensual mound, deep butt-crack parted, balls visible between his legs. His arms were folded under his head. He looked toward the doorway. He saw me. He saw me looking at him.

He rolled his hips, raised his ass, and his legs parted more. I saw into his crack. I saw his hole.

His lidded amber eyes stared at me. He rolled his ass again. An invitation.

I was so turned on I thought my dick would tear a hole in my jeans.

A flood of emotions, images, and self-examination hit me all at once. Powerful desire in the forefront, but also, as was my nature, I questioned my motives. Did I see what I wanted?

That ass, for sure. That body, for sure. But, more importantly, connection with someone I'd never met, someone who had no pre-conception of who I was. I could be anyone. He could be anyone.

And that someone obviously wanted me, wanted me to touch him, his naked butt, his naked body.

A total turn-on. The availability. The idea I could walk right in, right now, and seize his ass, spread it, touch it, finger it, lick it, fuck it!

I stared like a love-struck teen, and the guy grinned and winked. I wasn't actually drooling, but my desire was so obvious.

I stumbled away, some sense of practicality telling me I had to find my room first, take off my clothes, and look around the bath-house before I tumbled headfirst into a stranger's room—and ass.

Men brushed past me in the narrow corridor, some looking di-rectly at me, others averting their gaze. Someone groped my ass as they slid past. I found my room but not before I'd passed more open doorways, once glimpsing a pair of naked guys, one stroking a hard-on and the other lying back with legs up and cock, balls, and crack exposed.

It was all I'd fantasized.

I could barely strip fast enough in my impossibly small room. My hands shook and my hard-on bobbed and a fear nagged that my boner would show through my towel. As if it would be a bad thing in that environment.

I wrapped the towel around my waist and headed out, deter-mined to scout the place before I dove into one of the rooms for a wild bout of sexual fulfillment.

It was a meat market. Whether it was because it was a Friday night, or because it was always busy with hungry men on the prowl for sex, I could only guess.

I moved ahead on my quest for what mysteries lay ahead. I found a darkened room with a pair of television monitors playing nasty porn and a half-dozen men lounging on couches and benches. One guy was on his knees, sucking another guy's cock in front of everyone. Another guy had his cock out, long and pink and glistening, and stroked it while he alternately watched the cock-sucking show and the porn on the screens.

I searched out the showers. I wanted to be fresh and clean, yes, but I also wanted to be naked in front of the wandering crowd. I was a farm boy with a leanly muscled body, my ace in the hole. I'd get sex because I had a hot bod. I wasn't embarrassed to shower with other guys, but I was nervous about my near-constant hard-on.

Once I stood under the warm spray, and began to soap up, my embarrassment dissipated. A half-dozen guys inhabited the large tiled room, naked under the showers, half of them with stiffies, others checking out the stiffies.

A doorway in the corner led into a steam room, marked by the billowing clouds that escaped whenever someone entered or exited. I had to check it out.

The wall of moist heat smacked against my fresh-from-the-shower nudity. Near darkness. Heavy breathing. Moaning and sighing. A blur of bare flesh through the swirling steam.

I found my way to a tiled bench along the nearest wall. The darkness grew less impenetrable. There was someone on both my right and my left, one on a lower bench and the other beside me.

The tiles were slick with steam, sensual against my bare ass cheeks. My cock, already semi-stiff, reared up rampant as the background moans grew louder. I couldn't see across the room, but something warm, wet, and nasty was going on.

Something else warm grazed my bare thigh. A hand, from the guy on my right, boldly slid along the slippery muscle of my leg toward my crotch. I gasped, realizing I'd been holding my breath, as the hand grasped the base of my cock. I dared a glance at him.

Through the steam: dark hair and eyes, strong features, a wide mouth open, tongue out. I groaned as his hand began to pump, lifting my butt slightly off the tiles to thrust into his hand.

A second hand slid up my other leg from below. The other guy! The fingers of his hand were quick to zero in on my crotch, under my balls, probing my crack. I lifted my butt and raised, opening wide for exploring fingers.

I gasped. Heat rushed from my gut into my head. Not just from the steam, or from those intimately groping hands, but from my own brazen willingness to engage in anonymous, semi-public sex. A finger slipped past my trembling sphincter and into my ass.

I gripped behind my knees and pulled back. I spread myself open and grunted as I was finger-fucked, while another hand pumped up and down my aching cock.

After a few steamy minutes, I had to break away, gasping as I stumbled to my feet. I was on the verge of orgasm, but not ready for release. We had not exchanged a word. I left the steam room.

The hallways beckoned, as did the first ass I'd encountered an hour, or an eon, earlier. I wanted to lay on top of that naked man, thrust into him with my stiff cock, fuck him, fondle him, kiss him, stroke him.

My search was punctuated by impromptu hallway gropes, as bolder customers tweaked my nipples, grabbed at my towel-covered crotch and ass, or whispered offers of wild sex back in their cubicles.

Although not exactly shy, I was reticent to initiate encounters. So I paused at rooms, peering in, but was unable to drive my hesitant feet into the promised land of naked male sex.

The doorway to the first ass I coveted was closed. I didn't see it— or him—in the hallways, television room, or the darkened corners where others slurped and grunted and groped.

It didn't matter in the end. I found a similar ass, round and smooth and inviting. A blond guy, relaxed, eyes intent, a half-smile of welcome, lying on his belly, legs wide open. I stared, a deer in the headlights, unable to move away or to step inside.

He slid a pale hand over his own ass cheek. I bit my lip, mesmerized as he pulled it open and exposed his pink hole.

"It's all yours, buddy. Come on in."

The whispered invitation hooked me.

He laughed as I slammed the door and whipped off my towel. I glanced at his face, offering a tentative smile before I dove into his ass, face first.

I ate him out. He squirmed and mewled. I barely held back orgasm as I tongued and licked his crack and hole. He held his butt cheeks wide for me, rearing up to meet my mouth with his ass.

I fucked him. Lying on top of his lean body first, then doing him on his hands and knees, and then rolling him over and kissing his sweet mouth as I pumped him full of cock.

We talked afterward. I don't recall his name, and I never saw him again. But we laughed together, shared secrets, touched each other tenderly. It was a relaxing interlude, but after a while I was ready for more exploring. He understood.

Wandering, gawking like the naïve country boy I was, amazed at the blatant reek of desire and bold admission of lust, I reveled in the allure of expectation. What would happen next? I had no idea.

Another encounter, another orgasm, and I thought I was satiated. But as I showered off the sweat of a stranger, I realized there was one more desire I wanted to satisfy that night.

In my room, I stripped off the towel with shaking hands, and positioned the open door so that a view of my small bunk was unobstructed. Lying down on my stomach, I folded my hands under my head, turned my face so I could watch the doorway, and spread my legs to show off my farm-muscled ass and powerful legs. My asshole pulsed. My cock throbbed under my belly.

I waited. Guys wandered past, stopping to check me out, eyes on my firm ass, my sturdy legs, my broad back, my muscled arms. I recalled the first ass I had seen earlier, imagining how he felt, waiting, available, on display.

I basked in the moment. All around me, men were engaging in a free-for-all of sexual adventures. I was part of it, for real, at last.

Never again would I fear it was impossible. On that night, in the steamy bathhouse of desires, I was liberated.

The Signal is Jammed: A Confession

Mark Ambrose Harris

I found my desire within the hum of electricity and other sound waves.

Having grown up without cable television, I was stuck with the standard handful of local channels in Montreal, Canada. During my final years of adolescence, cable eventually made its way into my home. I am not sure how or when, but at some point I discovered the wonder of late-night scrambled porn. Since I was still living with my parents, I would plug my earphones into the television jack to keep the volume discreet, and I would try to make out the occasional body part on the flickering screen. I admit, I was not entirely into the straight porn that the cable company was transmitting, but it was all I had access to at that time.

Then, one Monday night, the satellites and the planets aligned. I changed the channel to Showcase and discovered that *Queer as Folk*, a British show I had read about, was premiering on Canadian television. While I had previously seen some light adult content during after-hours CBC films, including a penis or two, nothing could prepare me for this. I was stunned; never had I seen such explicit man-on-man action! My body felt oddly cold, and my limbs were tense, like when you have been awake for too long but feel far from tired. Vibrating inside of me was this untapped erotic energy that began to swell at the first sight of my own desire reflected back at me. Of course, looking back, what I was witnessing on television was an extremely hermetic version/vision of same-sex desire: very thin, very white, very affluent, and hairless. However, for a young queer who was still a virgin, and who had never even kissed another man, this first glimpse at what penetrative gay sex might look like was a paramount shift in understanding my own sexuality. As the night went on, and my hard-on ached like never before, I went channel surfing for something X-rated, for something scrambled. Once again, I stumbled upon a very important discovery—every Monday night, one of the adult film channels featured gay porn.

Monday nights became an opportunity to let my imagination billow and to amass more fantasies. After all, imagination is the key ingredient to watching scrambled porn. In fact, it may be the best part. There are people who say that the aim of consuming scrambled porn is to catch that brief moment when the image lapses and everything becomes clear. In retrospect, however, I preferred to watch bodies move in quivering swirls and static blips, cocks and asses pulsing shades of electric blue, torsos and backs fluctuating between cyan and indigo, eyes and teeth inverted to the negative, men hugging, kissing, rimming, fingering, sucking, and fucking in a hypercolored landscape.

As these rippling colors flooded my eyes, tiny earphones filled my ears with the sounds of everything I could not see. The divide between image and audio in pornography was perhaps most evident to me during those Monday nights. Living in Quebec, the movies were all originally filmed in English, and then dubbed into French. Therefore, I knew that voice actors had faked the scant dialogue, as well as the moans, the groans, the panting, the heavy breathing, and the sucking and slurping noises for the sake of the overdub. Again, imagination is integral to scrambled porn, and perhaps to porn in general. Either way, I was content to pretend that those intimate sounds were real, and that the aural eroticism could tell more of a story than the swaying image.

When I watched scrambled porn nearly a decade ago, it was as though the sex was being performed by creatures that were post-human, forms that had experienced drastic genetic mutation, limbs stretching, expanding, morphing, changing shape, and skin undulating hues with chameleon precision. While the original signal was mainstream adult film, it was not the monolith of pornography that informed my arousal. I was not bombarded by images of waxed buff plumbers, army men, cops, repairmen, naughty students, and strict teachers with unorthodox disciplinary methods. Instead, I went exploring in a kaleidoscopic world inhabited by cerulean, alien flesh. However, now that we have witnessed the end of analog television in an era of planned obsolescence, and Internet pornography has become a ubiquitous leviathan, it is as though the surrealist scrambled bodies have died off. The possibilities that the kinetic Technicolor body had to offer is extinct. The mystery is gone. There are times when the porn on my computer has not downloaded properly, and some pixels appear corrupted or missing. Sex becomes jagged and pixilated, geometric and digital. This is a reminder that computers now transform the pornographic body into rigid binary code within the limbic core of the machine.

Due to the deep body memory I have of those Monday nights, I prefer to consume my digital porn wearing earphones. Sometimes this reminds me of gamblers who cannot tear themselves away from playing the slots, their money cards in the machines, the cards attached to their torsos with a clip and a wire. It looks as though no monetary transactions are taking place, but the prosthetic umbilical cords say otherwise. Of course, the earphones-as-sex-toy is not pernicious, like the veins that draw money and blood from casino patrons. Nonetheless, I do recognize that there is something post-flesh about employing earphones to get off. I place a small piece of machinery in my ear, inside my body, and a wire connects me to the computer. The hard drive then broadcasts a sound wave into me, causing the most minuscule bones in my body—the stirrup, the anvil, and the hammer—to vibrate.

There is something that I have not yet brought up, which might seem like a glaring oversight for anyone who has ever watched an adult film: what I like to call porn Muzak, otherwise known as the pornographic soundtrack. Even back when I was sitting in the covert darkness of my basement watching sex flicks, there was something about porn soundtracks that irked me. Beyond the outdated synthesizer key sounds and the hackneyed drum lines, it was the looping that I found irritating. Due to lackluster editing, I could hear the abrupt jump-cut as a music loop would end and immediately start over. The repeat was far from seamless. Not only that, but I began hearing porn scores being reused in multiple films. As hard as I tried to fantasize that the frequencies I was receiving were authentic, the recycled Muzak was always on the verge of disrupting the sonic mirage. The soundtracks called attention to the façade of realism that is porn, but worse than that, the music often masked the voices and dialogue of the bioluminescent electric blue beings.

On those Mondays so many years ago, I used to hope that the nightly movie would not feature any music, so that I could better hear the actors' voices and bodily sounds. Again, while I was aware that most of the audio had been overdubbed, it was the human soundtrack, unhampered by porn Muzak, which I found arousing. The bodily noises felt unbridled and unmediated, vocalizations being the litmus of the scene's intensity when the television screen divulged nothing. Yet, dialogue was also quite stimulating to my queer imagination. I am certainly not the first person to comment on the vapid scripts of the pornographic genre. Overdubbed or not, most porn dialogue acts in tandem with its musical accompaniment: it loops. Repetition is not due to a technical aspect of sound editing, but to the actors' delivery and catch phrases. Endless cycles of "You like that? You like that? You like that?" or "Suck that dick … yeah … suck that dick … yeah … Suck that dick …" become tiresome to the point of comedy. Even here, on paper, the script lines do not appear remotely erotic, but rather, mechanical and unimaginative.

When I first began to write about sound in adult films, I was struck by the memory of my virgin self, watching scrambled porn and being turned on mostly by what I was hearing. I had forgotten about those Monday nights. Since starting this process of writing about my relationship with the audible male body of gay porn, I now realize the capacity for language to function as a fetish object. I recognize that in some ways, the kind of bedroom talk found in triple-X flicks has shaped my desire. I still find myself turned on by words, the intonations, the phrasing, and the grain of the voice. Moreover, I must confess that even some of the dialogue truisms are guaranteed to get me hard. As much as I may lambaste porn soundtracks, I admit that I like having sex to music by artists that nod to the porno aesthetic, such as Khan, and his magnificent sleazy post-lounge album *1-900-Get-Khan* in particular. Hearing a bass frequency that feels as though it wants to bleed out of the stereo and devour me is a definite aphrodisiac. There are many critiques to be made of pornography, and perhaps some might find it troubling that this film genre has informed my understanding of my sensuality and myself. However, it is not the purpose of this essay to pick at the cracks in porn's sweaty veneer. I would rather focus on the power of fantasy and imagination that is, perhaps, still possible in watching people fucking on screen. I would rather concentrate on the fact that scrambled porn has put me in tune with a part of my sexuality that may have otherwise remained dormant. I have managed to leave my gaze behind and instead turn to sound's ability to stimulate the body.

When we hear someone sing, we are listening to how sound resonates in their body. When we listen to a singer, we hear their skull, teeth, diaphragm, lungs, saliva, bones, and muscle. The voice in song is just one way we get to hear the intimate tales of the body. Consider the vocal rhythms of someone experiencing sexual pleasure. The sounds of the inner recesses are brought outwards, which makes pornographic audio almost hyper-intimate. In a moan, I hear diaphragm and lungs. In a grunt, I hear teeth and tongue. Furthermore, the technology of recording equipment and strategic microphone placement permit a field of extreme sonorous voyeurism. I hear orifices, up close, being pried open by fingers, dildos, butt plugs, and cocks, spit dripping from full mouths, balls slapping against asses, the slip of genitals against genitals through a thin layer of lubricant, the scream of leather against skin, the swan song of the orgasm. The pornographic image places a translucent barrier between the screen and my eyes. However, X-rated sound via a headset brings the scene directly into my body. Wires, filaments, circuit boards, and microchips send organic orgasmic noises into the realm of my fantasy.

Headphones enable pornography for the ear.

Ball One, or How I Learned to Stop Worrying and Love Baseball

Wayne Hoffman

I sucked at baseball when I was a kid.

I didn't know how to swing a bat, and I invariably flinched when a pitch came flying my way. I was too chubby to round the bases with any grace. And, of course, I threw like a girl—specifically, a dorky, uncoordinated girl with some sort of tragic physical impairment.

At school we had to play sports, but I could always opt out of baseball for something else, usually an athletic endeavor the teachers had intended for the actual girls: field hockey, gymnastics, speed walking. (Yes, speed walking, and don't laugh—it's the only "sport" where I excelled, waddling my way to the front of the pack.) I figured it was better to have the boys tease me for two minutes each day when we first chose our sports than to have them laugh at me for an hour solid while they watched me make a fool of myself on the baseball field.

At home, I spent most of my time inside, in the basement. That's where we kept the board games, the Ping-Pong table, the Chinese checkers—anything that might allow a kid to pass the time in a sports-free environment with one of his equally dorky, uncoordinated friends.

The basement was where my dad stashed his *Playboy* magazines. He thought he'd hidden them pretty well in his study, under a bunch of junk in the back of a drawer in a dresser that nobody used. But boys can sniff out porn before they've learned to tie their shoes.

I had been flipping through my dad's *Playboy*s since third or fourth grade—usually at the urging of other boys whose fathers didn't keep such magazines in their homes. I must have been around ten or eleven when one of my friends and I sat down on the floor in the study to check out the latest issue. He was pointing out which models had the biggest "boobs" and pretending to understand the party jokes as I nodded along beside him. And then, in the turn of a page, I fell in love.

Growing up in Maryland, even as an unathletic kid, I certainly knew who Jim Palmer was. Star pitcher for the Baltimore Orioles, he'd broken all sorts of records and was forever being interviewed on the local television news. He was well-spoken, widely respected, and idolized by baseball fans from Chesapeake Bay to the Potomac River.

But here, in the pages of *Playboy*, was a Jim Palmer I had never known. A Jim Palmer who wore Poco briefs.

He stood tall in the half-page ad, his unbuttoned plaid Oxford shirt open wide enough to reveal a lean and hairy torso, as well as the Jockey label on his low-rise Pocos. He was lit dramatically, deep shadows obscuring half of his face and bringing the contents of the unique two-layer pouch into bold relief.

I made a mental note of the page number and went back to feigning interest in the playmate of the month.

In the coming months, I realized that the pitcher had been hired as a pitchman for Jockey's whole line of underwear. Each new issue of *Playboy* featured a different ad.

Building on the designer jeans craze of the early 1980s, Jockey put a shirtless Palmer in the new jeans briefs: denim-blue, no-fly underwear with contrast stitching. His classic *Thinker* pose struck a perfect contrast to the "contemporary" briefs.

Still trying to hold on to more traditional customers, Jockey soon put him in standard issue tighty-whities: a crew neck undershirt tucked into the company's trademark Y-front briefs. Timeless.

And in my favorite ad, Jockey put the pitcher in blue-and-white striped Elance briefs, the "fashionable" kind sold in a tube. He was seated in this ad, one leg propped up and one arm akimbo, as it was in almost every ad—just like the jockey in the company's logo. His long legs were spread slightly, the horizontal stripes of the briefs revealing every contour of his exposed crotch.

I made a written list of which page in which issue contained which ad, and took to visiting my father's study at every possible opportunity, whether my friends were visiting or not.

Then I realized that Jockey was running ads in the *People* magazines my mother kept stacked on her nightstand. While my father saved his *Playboys*, my mother threw out her *Peoples* every few weeks, and I found that by sneaking down to the garbage, I could clip and save my favorite Jockey ads. I started a collection.

At night, in my bedroom, I'd spread the clipped ads across my comforter and fantasize about a dozen Jim Palmers at once. A whole wall of hairy chests, a forest of muscular arms, an endless sea of soft cotton pouches filled to capacity.

Palmer looked old enough to be my father. But my dad was no all-star athlete. Besides, he wore fuddy-duddy Hanes, stretched out and dingy, always the same. Nothing with stripes. Nothing that came in a tube. He was no competition for my favorite Oriole.

I became obsessed.

For a short time, I took to scanning the sports pages in the morning, looking for more pictures of Palmer to cut out, but the photos weren't nearly as revealing, and all the sports writers talked about was his ERA—which was not the kind of statistic that interested me.

When Jockey unveiled its Jockey for Her line of women's underwear, my mother and sister went to the store to buy a few items. With their first purchase they got a free gift: an autographed color poster of Palmer reclining in light-blue bikinis. I wanted to hang the damn thing on the ceiling over my bed so I could look at it every night, but I couldn't figure out a way to ask for it without raising eyebrows. So my sister took it. The worst part? She kept it rolled up in her closet, instead of putting it on her wall where I could at least have sneaked a peek at it.

Eventually, I expanded my underwear ad collection to include anyone else I could find: middle-aged men in Montgomery Ward's Sunday circulars, Fruit of the Loom models from magazines, muscular guys wearing designer briefs in Bloomingdale's promotions. I pasted the ads together into homemade catalogs, crude versions of my father's *Playboy*s. But clear through junior high, Jim Palmer was my playmate of the month.

In later years, I discovered real porn, where the men didn't wear anything at all. I moved on, and so did Palmer: He retired from baseball, stopped posing half-naked, and became famous instead as a shill for The Money Store in television ads.

But after all this time, his signature is still evident in my erotic imagination. I can see it today in my ongoing fascination with older men, in my almost Pavlovian response—drooling, panting, occasional barking—at the sight of chest hair, in my fetish for men's briefs, even though I've always worn boxers. Those things haven't changed since I first saw Jim Palmer in his Jockey shorts.

One other thing hasn't changed, either. I'm still a terrible baseball player. But sometimes, nowadays, I do like to watch.

The Weight of My Desire

Christopher DiRaddo

I used to see you at Sky every weekend, at the bar, with your friends.
I was there by myself in those days. Just a kid in sneakers and a
tight T-shirt, mesmerized by the zany circus rollicking around me.
I remember the night I was kissed by a strange boy from Boston,
and the time Madame Simone came up to me sporting a ridiculous
dildo on her dress, bobbing up and down on the dance floor to
"Blue Monday." She always made me crack a smile. Otherwise, I
was stone-faced. Life was so serious for me back then. I went out
alone because I didn't know anyone. I'd grab a beer and find a corner from which to watch the world.

I had such a crush on you in those days. All I knew was your
name and that you studied at Concordia. You were tall and slender,
with long pale arms and pink, pinched elbows.

You were by the dance floor the first time I saw you. You wore a
trucker shirt and baseball cap, with a thin gold chain around your
neck. You walked over and stood beside me, looking not at me but
at the men dancing. I was transfixed by your proximity, by the heat
of your body. I was flushed and woozy. Fantasies filled my head. I
wanted so much to grab you, absorb the warmth of your skin. But
back then a part of me still believed that nobody shared my passion
for men—even in a bar buzzing with homos.

One of the first people I ran into at a gay bar that I knew was
Marco, an athletic French-Canadian who had been in my senior
year of high school. He was better known in those bar days as Cameron, an occasional go-go dancer who also stripped down the street
at one of the Village's less reputable establishments. "I'm not gay,"

he had told me, self-righteously, the night I bumped into him by the bathroom. "I'm just doing this for the money." And I believed him. Marco had always used his body to get what he wanted from the girls in our school. I had tried hard not to stare at him in class: a plump forearm resting so certainly on a textbook, solid thighs disappearing into tight gym shorts. I thought he was the type of guy who'd bust my face for looking at him the wrong way. Instead, he wanted me to pay for looking.

I have never understood gay sexual desire for straight men, why so many of us revel in tales of homoerotic horseplay in locker rooms, why some of us pay monthly Internet memberships to watch two buddies who won't kiss poke their cocks at each other in front of a camera. I suppose we hope that these guys might secretly like it, that, given a lick, those buddies might find themselves in our beds. Or maybe it's a revenge fantasy, a chance for us to get back at the straight boys who recognized, and then ridiculed, our desire for them. Or perhaps it's a way to play out those unrequited attempts at hookups with friends in our youth. But whatever the reason, I don't share the pervasive desire for a straight boy. Nor did I feel the need to check out Cameron's show down the street. No, these men are indifferent to, or want nothing to do with, our lust for them, and I have never found that reluctance attractive.

I like men. And I like that I like men. But more than that, I like that you like them too. I mean, you do like them, don't you? Why else did I see you at the bar as often as I did, watching, with the same rapt attention as mine, an endless parade of male youth? Sometimes, I think, the only thing greater than my desire for a man is my desire for his hunger. Do you know what I mean? His yearning to touch, or be touched by, another man. His willingness. His lust. His lack of inhibition. The thought that maybe just the hook of another man's smile is enough to get him hard. That perhaps even you might think of me and quiver. That I might hold the power to do that to you. Then I could pull you close, press your forehead into mine, and gaze into your eyes as we fuck. And in your eyes I will see that you like it. I will hear it on your warm breath and in the wet sound of your tongue on my skin. We are not that different, you and I. Your balls ache the way mine do.

I tried to talk to you once, but failed miserably. This was weeks, perhaps months, later. We were at Sky again, and I was watching from a corner as you sat with your friend on the windowsill by the pool table. I drank nervously from my bottle, snacking on peanuts, trying to get up the nerve to talk to you. I thought about what I could say that wouldn't be corny or inappropriate, that would grab your attention and open up a conversation. About school? Or this bar? Or the queer sense of self I had begun to discover? Would you understand what I was trying to say? Would I be articulate? Or clumsy and odd?

Or I could say nothing, finish my beer, go home. But I did that all the time. And then felt crappy about denying my attraction, about not speaking up for what I wanted. So on that night, though shy and frightened, I decided that if I were to go home feeling insignificant and dejected, it would be because I had been shot down, not because I hadn't tried.

I waited by the stairway for your friend to leave, to order another beer, to go to the washroom, to do something—anything—that would leave you alone for just one moment. I was anxious, the music was loud, and I was sure people were staring at me. I sipped beer, swallowed peanuts, and fretfully checked my watch a dozen times. I caught the eye of an older man nearby, amused by my anxiety. Then your friend moved to the bar.

After one more sip of courage, I moved toward you, stopping a few feet from where you sat, your face in profile, oblivious as always that I was standing close ...

I stood there. Mute.

You didn't turn, didn't acknowledge my presence. I tried to speak, but gasped instead, choking on half-swallowed peanuts. You turned to look at me as your friend arrived, two beers in hand. Puzzled, you spoke. "Hello?"

Those seconds between my gasp and your words were an eternity, during which I closed down, went blank. Nothing about you or me or anything I might have ever thought about the two of us was at all possible. So used to the indifference of straight boys in my youth, I had trouble believing in the possibility of us. I could not ask for what I so ardently desired.

I know I should have tried. My words might have come out in a sputter, or as small talk, an insignificant conversation about weather or studies. What I wanted to tell you, but could not, was that you made me happy.

Well, not you, because I didn't know you. But the idea of you. The word you. And the idea of you and me. You represented the other half of the sexual equation I was trying to decipher—a pairing that added up to a we. A ripe we that I wanted so much to pluck and devour for days.

But I don't think you would have understood me, so instead of saying what I longed to say, I mumbled an, "Excuse me, I'm sorry," and cut across the bar to the exit. The older man laughed to himself—or at me—as I left.

I never tried to speak to you again after that awkward encounter. Soon I met someone to pair up with, and I didn't think about you much anymore (although I never quite forgot you). Years later, though, I understood finally why I was not able to communicate my desire for you, to you.

It was because it would have meant something. Over the years I have had so much small talk with men in bars. We've talked about nothing and anything, about the price of the beer, the paint on the walls, the buff bartender. But what I wanted to say to you that night carried with it the weight of my youth, my questions, my confusion, my dreams. I wasn't bearing the weight of the walls of the bar as I leaned against them, watching you; I was bearing the weight of my desire for a man, perhaps any man. And I had rested it solely upon you.

Noble Failures: A Catalog of One-Night Stands (1994–1998)

Viet Dinh

Harris T.: Nebbish. Jewish. Sat quietly in a gay men's group in Baltimore. A thick five o'clock shadow crept up from his chest and along his neck, dark and rough as iron filings. His mother used to call him "Harrisol," both endearing and odd. Owned a townhouse near the Inner Harbor. At the end of our evening, asked, "So, do we make out now?" Why bother asking? Had me sleep alone in an unheated guest room, where I pulled the comforter around me, an acrylic cocoon, and curled into the fetal position. The next morning, got cross with me when I passed by a freshly poured slab of pavement and wrote my initials in the wet concrete with my finger. Didn't understand that I just wanted to leave a mark.

Kent M.: On paper, the perfect man. Medical doctor, handsome, hair in curls that resisted my fingers' best efforts to straighten them. Talked about hang-gliding. Incessantly: at the Chihuly exhibit at the Baltimore Museum of Art, over dinner, back at his townhouse where his hang-gliding apparatus stood propped in the entryway like a pinned butterfly. Had dreams about making love while hang-gliding, of ecstasy in freefall. I was afraid of heights.

Ralph B.: German grad student at the University of Maryland. Wore glasses, studied computer science, knew me from the *#gay dc* IRC chat room. Also favored, as I learned later, the *#gay piss* room. After dinner at Shoney's, took me back to his host family's home. The host mother, who filled her home with Native American art and kept her hair in unruly dreads, knew exactly what was going on; looked at me as if this had happened before. A bread machine whirred in the background, and the smell of rising dough trailed down to his basement room. But I was better flirting as a disembodied persona; I preferred listening to his Teutonic accent than my own voice.

Scott H.: Short and balding, but with a wiry strength. Charming. An acquaintance from around DC. I had a crush on him for the longest time and had told my friends about it. They teased me whenever I grew tongue-tied in his presence. Seemed to take things in stride, in good-humor—must have heard about my crush from my friends. Took me, one warm spring afternoon, on a drive down Rock Creek Parkway in his dying red Porsche convertible, the gearbox grinding with each shift. Let me spend the night, as if to satisfy my curiosity—or perhaps to satisfy his own. Stayed friends until I reluctantly let my crush fade.

Jason W.: English teacher. Originally from North Carolina, but had meticulously scrubbed his speech free of any accent. Had two cats: Comma and Apostrophe. Asked me what I wanted. At that moment or in general? I wouldn't have had an answer either way. Led me away from his bookcase, where I looked at the titles stacked on the shelves as if I could understand him better by what he read. Blindfolded me with a necktie that he wore while teaching, and asked again, "What do you want?"

Calvin D.: A cinderblock of a man; my arms wouldn't fit all the way around him. Worked in construction but painted murals on the side. Murals for nurseries: rainbows, fluffy clouds, teddy bears, and picnics. Just as our intimacy started, said, "I can't. My boyfriend." The first I'd heard of this boyfriend. The boyfriend (out of town) had been taking medicine that drained him of libido. Paxil? Zoloft? Prozac? Told me about his aunt in Shreveport—while I lay in bed

next to him, legs dangling off the side, pants around my ankles—
and described his recurring dream of praying mantises coming out
of her eyes.

Cary G.: Development director for the Whitman-Walker clinic. Ar-
tificially inflated the bids at a charity auction that he was conduct-
ing. Noticed me raising an eyebrow and winked at me. Led me to
the roof of my apartment building, because the summer air outside
was cooler than my un-air-conditioned studio. Held my hand as
DC moved below us, the couples tracing paths to and from Dupont
Circle, the single people, the life that I could see but not connect
with. Talked about how much he disliked working for nonprofits
and about moving to California.

John R.: Former philosophy major, now health informatics grad student, with strawberry blond hair. Laughed at an obscure Thomas
Aquinas joke. Stood about five inches taller than me, hovered above
me like a canopy. Spoke incessantly about his ex, had only recently rented out the recently vacated room, and looked at me as if I
should have been someone more familiar. I should have recognized
these signs. Pulled away as I tried to pull closer, and I don't know
which was more surprising, that he never called again or that I had
expected him to.

Theodore K.: Loved obscure *giallo* films and their soundtracks.
Pulled at the individual bristles in his beard. Discussed his work,
about how inertia held him in place, when what he really wanted to
do was move to Europe. The more he talked about work, the more
a dark cloud formed around him. Preferred wearing beige clothing
that made him indistinguishable from the wall—but didn't wear
underwear. Absorbed in his own thoughts, smiled shyly and rarely,
but those moments were so bright that I wanted, if only for a moment, to take him out of his head and into the present, where I
could serve as a distraction for both of us.

Leo R.: Fuzzy shaved head. Slender as a sidelong whisper. Deaf. Wrote notes to me on a napkin, which we passed back and forth, and when that napkin had filled, took me to his apartment. Showed me a commercial for the United Way in which he had appeared. Had a full head of dark, curly hair in the video in which he signed the lyrics to "I Can See Clearly Now." Spoke with his hands, an indecipherable marvel. They swirled around each other. The fingers of his left hand blossomed, and he rubbed his outstretched palm with his right hand. How does one master the two languages of a body? There was the one to which I responded instinctually, the conversation of blood beneath the skin, and the one which I could never understand.

John S.: Late November. Loved apples. Cut slices of a Honeycrisp with a paring knife in his apartment and fed them to me before the flesh had a chance to turn brown. Sent me home with a half-gallon of apple cider that he'd bought that morning at the farmer's market. Quiet and unassuming, slightly pudgy. Tilted his head down whenever he smiled as if embarrassed. Worked in the acquisitions department of Johns Hopkins' library.

From his window, I saw Wyman Park at night, a loop around the Baltimore Museum of Art, a notorious cruising spot. I took note of the cars that passed by once, twice—again and again, searching the shadows with their headlights. I wondered where the others were, the park's nocturnal denizens, hustlers, and fellow lonely souls. The dark underworld of men willing to risk their livelihoods, their lives, for an evening of pleasure, of connection. Then I remembered who I was, where I was. That I was no different.

Truth was, as kind and as gentle as John was, as much as I appreciated his apple cider, even though I had to lay the jug sideways to fit it in the refrigerator of my studio apartment, I knew that this would hurt him more than it would hurt me. And I was okay with that. He wouldn't learn until later—when I had to explain, awkwardly, why I wouldn't see him any more—that I was coming off a relationship, that my emotions were in a tailspin. He accepted this, and I never heard from him again.

I should have been more forthright with my intentions, my desires, but there are things you don't say in order not to hurt another person—or yourself. It's easier to wrap your tongue around another's than to shape vocal expressions of want and need and desire. Of course, it's easy to say these things years later, from a silent distance, but in that moment, lost, insulated by the sheets, staring up at the dark ceiling, listening to the story about the first time John ever dropped acid, licking the ooze of apples still sticky on your fingers, you say what seems right, what feels good, and that is almost never "I'm sorry."

Straight Guy Fetish

Rob Wolfsham

After huffing up three flights of stairs, I walked into apartment 334, where the party clattered along in full swing. At least forty people milled about the cramped eighteen-by-twenty-foot living room and connecting kitchen, talking loudly over music, laughing, holding red cups. Tenacious D blared from a stereo. Several guys stood around the speaker cabinets, singing along with the rock opera jaunts of "Fuck Her Gently," pumping their fists.

My roommate Stephanie—a tall red-haired girl, my best friend— stood behind the kitchen counter pouring shots of tequila. She bartended at Skooners, where we frequently hung out. She glanced at me as I walked in, then said nonchalantly, "Rob, look out."

A man rammed me from behind, arms bear-hugging me. I tumbled to the carpet, falling to my hands and knees, a heavy body atop my torso. Clusters of people parted to make room for us on the floor. Noisy conversations continued. His arms rolled me sideways, swinging me onto him, my back on his chest. My head fell onto his shoulder. My cheek rubbed his bristly cheek, curtained in long blond hair.

"Guys, don't knock beer on the carpet," Peter said from the couch. Red cups covered the table in front of him, half obscuring us. A Ping-Pong ball landed in a cup, splashes of beer rained on my face—a Shiner Bock facial already, and I had only been at the party for thirty seconds.

Blond hairy arms locked me into a rear-naked chokehold. A finger wiggled into my ear. I groaned and squirmed. It wasn't a fluttering wet-willy, just a methodical poking.

"Hi, Kyle," I said.

"Hi," he said into my other ear, then pumped his hips once against my ass, popping me up a little.

"I don't know where your finger has been," I mumbled, my chin fighting his forearm.

"You take it," he commanded and humped me in the air again, jeans slapping. "You take it and you like it."

"Sure, I like when you stick your finger in my hole."

Kyle whined like a kid who just stepped in mud. "Gross." He pulled out his finger and licked it. "You taste good," he said matter-of-factly.

"And you say I'm gross?" I shifted and tried to pull his arm from my neck. It tightened. The red light of a camera trained on us, then a flash.

Stephanie laughed and reviewed the photo on the tiny screen. "You guys set yourselves up for embarrassing Facebook photos."

"I'm not even drunk yet," I protested. "Here, retake the photo with me rolling my eyes back. Can I get dry-humped again?"

He pushed me off. "How about no."

"Tease."

"Rob, take a tequila shot." Steph handed me a little glass.

I threw it back, liquid fire soothed with the bite of a lime slice. I shuddered and shook my head like a dog.

Peter wiped splashes of beer from the table. "Don't worry, Rob, he'll come around some day." I tossed the glass up to Steph.

Kyle sat up. "Fuck you. I just like messing with my Robby." He scratched my back.

I smacked his arm away. He tackled me to the floor again and grabbed my leg, pulling it under his arm in an ankle lock.

"Easy, easy!" I yelled.

He tightened, hyper-extending my ankle. I wailed, pain shooting up my leg, but the alcohol started its journey through my blood, straight to the sting.

"Jesus, Kyle, leave him alone," Peter said.

Stephanie flashed another picture, rotating around for better angles.

"He likes it," Kyle growled.

I looked back at Peter upside-down, a triangle of red cups on the table hanging over his black-bearded chin like a crown. "That's the secret," I said yawning in pain at him. "Reverse psychology is his gay kryptonite."

"He likes being challenged," Peter said as Kyle sulked. "You need a beer." He picked up a cup from the table and came down toward me.

"I don't want gross beer-pong beer."

Kyle swung around while clutching my leg, pulled it back over my head, and pivoted my butt into the air, so my crotch was hanging over my face. My chin dug into my chest. "This is awkward," I said, my voice muffled.

Kyle held my feet to the floor, put his bottle of Shiner to my lips, and tilted it. I suckled the bottle like I was trying to suck myself off. The barley taste of good Texas beer soothed my tongue as my throat struggled to swallow.

"This is really gay," a guy said, monotone. It sounded like Jacob.

I shut my lips against the bottle. Kyle tilted it more. Beer dribbled down my lips and through my goatee. I didn't really care. "So, come be gay with us," I said.

Jacob laughed and protectively put his arm around Stephanie. "I'll leave it to the experts."

Kyle let go of my leg and I unraveled and splayed out, stretched muscles and back getting a chance to rest. He sucked down the rest of his beer.

Jacob popped open a bottle and set it in my hand.

I sat up. "Thanks. I need about five more of these to keep up with Kyle's gayness." I chugged as his fist punched my arm.

It didn't take long until we were all piss drunk. We were celebrating Peter landing an internship with BNSF, a railway company that services the Great Plains. We were seniors. The college yarn was spinning to its end on a needle of booze and Jello shots.

The apartment soon morphed from incandescent hangout to swirling black-light dance party. White teeth glowed and laughed, and shoelaces, shirt stripes, and baseball cap etchings fluoresced.

In a few weeks, we would disperse across the country like fire-crackers, sparks fizzling into distant black obscurity. People drew on the walls with colorful black-light paint, sketching penises and vaginas and random doodles as The Knife's "Silent Shout" thumped around us. Peter moped between dancers about the mess of spilled and smashed red cups and glowing carpet stains, but soon said, "fuck it," and got trashed enough not to care.

We were celebrating the twilight of college and the inner ring of our social circle. Stephanie was an art-history major going to Pennsylvania for grad school. Peter would be leaving for Kansas. Jacob was going to bootcamp in Oklahoma.

I was going nowhere with my English major. I was going to be stuck in Lubbock, Texas, the edge of American civilization, a drunken college merry-go-round, windy, dust-caked, surrounded by an endless 360-degree horizon of cotton fields and dipping pumpjacks. Maybe I should have stuck with journalism. I could have traveled the world.

"I'm not going anywhere," Kyle slurred to me later, when we were on his bed behind a shut door, bathed in the light of his computer monitor. He pulled my shoes off and took a foot into his hands and rubbed expertly, sending pleasure up my leg.

His knuckles plowed the center of my foot. His fingers weaved through my toes and flexed. He always liked my feet, saying I was the only person with feet he'd touch. I grabbed his foot and mim-icked his moves, and he drifted around me into a back massage, both our shirts tangled on the floor. His calloused rock-climber hands rubbed down my skinny spine and up my shoulder blades, kneading, fingertips tracing my bony ribs.

"When do you graduate?" I asked, lips against the sheets, trying to stifle satisfied drooling as he sat on me.

"Probably never," he said distantly.

We had been doing this for four years: Getting drunk and rowdy at parties, then physically trapping ourselves in an intimate but platonic cage. Everyone knew when we disappeared from a party—it was sort of a running joke that Kyle was gay for me ... or gay in general. But nothing ever happened between us.

Peter knew Kyle since high school and was almost certain he was gay. Hearing that from Peter enraged me. If Kyle were gay, he wouldn't have to be alone. I'd made myself available to him for so long. Kyle knew I was gay; surely he would have dived in by now.

It was torture. I'd wanted him from the day we first met in our dorm lobby, when I plopped down on a couch next to him and he smiled with big blue eyes and ran strong hands through his long blond hair, and after ten minutes of chat put his arm around me playfully. Everyone knew I liked him. They knew I had a pathetic puppy love for conflicted, crazy Kyle. We've been doing this song and dance for years; rough-housing, heated grappling, deep massages, and sleeping in the same bed at random parties. But no sex. No release. No consummation. I never tried to take it further. I was going to let Kyle initiate if he ever wanted to take it there; he would come to me. I was afraid of ruining the physical intimacy we did have, even if it never had a climax.

Pinned under Kyle, my mind went to freshman year, when everything was new and I wasn't jaded and bitter about what I didn't get to do in college. Kyle had massaged me like this freshman year. And sophomore year. And junior year. And we were doing it now. I reached back and caressed his knee.

"I should have never left Amy," he said.

I grimaced into the sheets, my hand paused on his knee, and he continued, "Man, you know, she was like the nicest girl."

"High school ended a long time ago," I said with finality.

"I know, but we had such a good relationship, we still do. We still talk on Facebook. I talked to her the other day, and you know what she told me?"

He was drunk.

"She said, 'I wish we had done more in high school.' Do you know how much it hurts to hear that now?"

And there I lay under him, my skin at his fingertips. Kyle and Amy never dated in high school. They were friends from church. Kyle never obsessed about her until he got to college. Peter told me this once, and I wasn't surprised. Any time Peter or Jacob pressured Kyle to talk to girls at a bar or club, Kyle would get drunk and just brood about the omnipotent Amy. She was his heterosexual handicap.

"Let go of it," I said to the sheets. "She's gone. She goes to OU. She has a boyfriend."

"She hates him. We could get back together."

"No. You can't."

He pinched my back over my left kidney, a horrible bite of pain. I growled and twisted under him.

Kyle seethed. "What do you know about straight love?"

"All my friends are straight. I have no gay friends. I've been a goddamn token watching all of you and your bullshit for four years."

Kyle started rubbing my back lightly again.

"No, stop." I writhed.

"What?"

"Why do you do this?" I pleaded and coiled around, and he got off of me and I flipped to my back, watching him.

"I don't know," he said in a distant, meek way, on his knees between my legs. "I like giving massages."

I propped up on my elbow and brought my hand to the side of his face and ran my fingers through his hair, down his neck, over his broad shoulder.

He pulled my hand away.

"Just let me return the favor," I said.

"Rob, I'm not—"

"Fuck the labels," I said. I was a little drunk too, but that was the wall between us: the word Amy and the word gay.

"You can sleep in my bed." He started to slide off the sheets, but I pulled him toward me by his shoulder, clumsy, pulling myself up toward him, toward his lips for something new and beyond the usual touch.

He resisted like a falling statue, edging out of my grip as if by gravity. I sat up and held his thigh and tried to kiss him and he flinched away, my lips lost in his hair. He grabbed my arm, pulling my hand off of him.

Rejection pounded me like thorny tumbleweeds in a West Texas windstorm, sixty-mile-per-hour winds sand-blasting my skin off. I let go, fell back on the bed, and stared at the plaster ceiling.

He sat on the side of the bed for a minute, then crawled onto the floor and passed out on the carpet next to his computer.

I couldn't decide if Kyle was just not ready, not ready to admit to himself what he liked, or if he was just some highly physical yet asexual creature. Or if I'm entirely vain and delusional, along with Peter and everyone else who said he was probably gay. Was Kyle a gay eunuch? Or was I just some straight guy's fetish? A punching bag for platonic male intimacy who won't reject or hurt him because I was desperate and isolated?

I woke up in the afternoon to the same post-party grogginess I had known for years. Wind howled outside the window, occasional bursts of sand sprayed the glass.

Kyle still slept, curled under his desk chair. He had his leather jacket wrapped around him like a blanket.

I walked out to the living room where Peter, Jacob, Stephanie, and some strangers were mumbling about where to eat. I didn't hear their good afternoons or their wink-winked "So how was last night?"

I went outside to the apartment's third-floor balcony. Roaring April wind and sand beat my face. The view of the shops on University Avenue and Texas Tech's campus stretched out before me,

Spanish architecture, brown bricks, and red-tiled roofs rising into a torrent of brown haze. I looked up until the brown curtains of dust and sand sifted into white, then a faint blue sky. I took a deep breath, inhaling the inhospitable wasteland out there, pulling it into me, pulling in something.

A year later, I'm poised to move into Kyle's new house, after landing a job at the university's museum. Most of our friends have graduated and we hardly speak anymore, but Kyle and I share the kinship of being stuck in Lubbock. It's been almost five years of cock teasing. I'll be fine with another five. The withholding is an exercise in platonic masochism.

Hairy Captives and Butch Bottoms

Jeff Mann

Joseph's where I've left him, lying on his side on our big bed, after-noon sun slanting over his hogtied nakedness. Yards of rough hemp rope cinch his elbows together, bind his upper arms to his torso, and tether his wrists and ankles tightly together behind his back.

"How you doing, cub?" I ask, standing in the doorway, studying the fur-matted curves of his chest and belly, thanking whatever gods brought us together. He nods happily, blinking up at me with long-lashed blue eyes.

Joseph's my boy: was there ever a bear cub more adorable? A short, compact, hairy guy, half my age and half my size, just the kind I love to top; he brings out in me that dangerous combination of paternal protectiveness, eager sadism, and doting tenderness that entirely enflames my libido and thoroughly seizes my heart.

Sitting on the bed's edge, I sip bourbon and tousle his wavy hair. "The stew'll be done in about an hour. I'll untie you then. Think you can take it that much longer?"

Joseph nods again, grinning around his ball gag. He's young and limber, in his mid-twenties; he can endure a lengthy bit of restraint, ardor, and abuse.

"You love it like this, don't you?" I say, kissing his moist brow.

"Uuuuuhhh-huh!" he murmurs, nodding again.

"Damn, I do too. You're beautiful this way." I stroke Joseph's neatly trimmed brown goatee; it's soaked with the copious drool a tightly strapped-in rubber ball evokes. He nuzzles my hand. Put-ting the glass of bourbon on the nightstand, I stretch out beside him. I kiss his gagged mouth; I lick his sodden goatee. Dropping my mouth to his nipples, I roughen them up with tongue and teeth, then stroke his bobbing erection with thumb and forefinger till he's panting and thrusting into my grip.

"You want the plug now?" I whisper.

More nodding, increasingly vigorous.

"On your belly."

Joseph obeys, rolling over and spreading his thighs as widely as his bonds allow. I kiss his beautifully furry ass cheeks, then part them and lube up his tightness with a finger, then two. "Thank you, Dad," he sighs into his gag, bucking back against my hand. When he's ready, I replace my fingers with the butt plug's lubed tip. By slow degrees, Joseph opens; by slow degrees, I gently work the plug inside, evoking long, low, ecstatic moans.

I rise, wiping my sticky fingers with Kleenex. Joseph makes a delicious spectacle, rocking back against the plug, humping the air. God, the boy loves to have his ass filled up. Later, I'll untie him, we'll share a good dinner, cuddle on the couch, and watch a movie. After that, I'll tie his hands behind his back, clamp his nipples, stuff the ball-gag back in his mouth, push him onto the bed, hoist his legs over my shoulders, and fuck him till he's hurting and we're both exhausted. He'll spend the night in my arms, contentedly helpless, comfortably bit-gagged, hands cuffed in front of him, steel shackles on his ankles. Tomorrow morning, waking before Joseph, I'll lie quietly beside him, studying his face and nakedness in the waxing light. My boy's so beautiful; it's the sweetest of gifts, watching him sleep.

Naked save for a worn jockstrap and chain-and-padlock slave collar, Sam's stretched out, arms pulled taut above his head, here in my basement gym. He grunts with discomfort as I hoist his hands higher until he's swaying on his toes. The rope binding his wrists together I've thrown over a ceiling pipe; now I anchor the rope's end to the weight bench. This should keep him firmly in place for the candlelit beating to come.

Sam's my slave: was there ever an otter hotter, more eminently fuckable? A lean, muscular, hairy guy in his forties, about my age, about my height, just the kind of butch country boy I love to top, he brings out in me that dangerous combination of fraternal solicitude, rough-edged cruelty, and tender adoration that entirely enflames my libido and thoroughly seizes my heart.

"Ready?" I say, standing before him, loving the way he pants and sways, the way expectation, surrender, and rapture fill his eyes and etch his handsome face. I run one hand over Sam's bare hip and another across his hairy pecs. I press my face into one musky, mossy armpit.

"Yep," he says, taking a deep breath. "Give it to me hard, Sir. I need it bad."

"You got it, boy," I say. The rag's rank—I've been pissing on it for days, as he'd requested. He gives me a little fight, tossing his head and gritting his teeth, before I force the balled-up cloth between his pretty lips. Just to keep the noise down further—for Sam will soon be making quite the pained fuss—I plaster a couple layers of duct tape over his goatee-framed mouth, smoothing the strips across his cheeks.

For a long minute we face one another in silence—kinky rednecks, Southern boys, captor and captive. I stroke his thinning hair and dark sideburns, I kiss the silvery tape across his mouth. When I wrap my arms around him, he leans against me, trembling and sighing. "Be strong for me, buddy," I say, slipping a blindfold over his eyes and leaving him to hang there in the sudden dark.

Time for the frat paddle. It's a heavy thing, solid oak, ordered from Mr. S, the leather store in San Francisco. Sam grunts under the first blow, teeters on his toes, then cocks his curvaceous and fuzzy ass in that precious position he always assumes when he's tacitly begging for more. He gets it. I beat him with steady but insistent force until he's yelping with each blow, my arm's aching, and his buttocks are bright red and beginning to bruise. We take a break, long enough for me to rope up his cock and balls with a thin cord, jack his dick until he's just this side of coming, and suck his hirsute nipples until he winces.

"More?" I ask. Sam nods, cocking his ass again. I lift the paddle and recommence. I won't stop until he's whimpering, until tears ooze beneath the blindfold and trickle down his duct-taped, stubble-rough cheeks. When he's had enough, I'll untether him from the pipe, push him over the weight bench, rope his hands behind him, spread his burning butt-cheeks, and eat his ass until he's begging me to rape him. I'll take Sam the way he loves it—hard, fast, rough—one hand clamped over his taped mouth, another tugging on his nipples and his cock. He'll shoot across the floor; I'll shoot inside him.

When I remove his bonds, gag, and blindfold, we'll lie together laughing, snuggling for a while on the gym mat. He'll mumble his thanks as I soothe his bruised ass with lotion. Then we'll head upstairs to mix drinks and collaborate on supper. I make a damned good foccacia, and his spaghetti sauce is legendary. My buddy/slave will spend the night nestling against me, contentedly helpless, with his hands tied in front of him and that piss-rag knotted loosely between his teeth. Tomorrow morning, when he nudges me awake, at his mumbled request I'll fuck him again. It's the sweetest of gifts, a bound and gagged slave like Sam, desperately eager to feel me inside him.

These parallel idylls with pseudonymous Joseph and Sam are, regrettably, fiction, not remembered fact. The BDSM erotica I write is, most often, pure wish fulfillment, the only way I can make love to beautiful men I cannot otherwise possess. Joseph is an ex-student, apparently straight, young enough to be my son, and most likely not into gay leather-play with Daddy Bears like myself. Sam is a famous heterosexual singer I've lusted after for years, who would probably be horrified by all the uses I've put him to in my fictions and fantasies. Joseph and Sam have already done their duty, so to speak, in several pieces of my published erotica, though

I must admit it was a pleasure to revisit them here.

It's a fairly fixed constellation, that combination of elements I find most arousing, most of them included in the scenes with Joseph and Sam described above. Like any fetishes, they might seem tediously repetitive to an outsider, but are endlessly fascinating to me, worth relishing in endless variation.

First, masculinity. Rural manhood in particular, since that's what I grew up around in the mountains of Virginia and West Virginia. (I am reactionary, I suppose, in finding most signifiers of traditional manhood appealing, but political correctness cannot, to be blunt, alter what makes me hard.) I love brown or black facial hair: beards, goatees, several-day stubble. I love dark body hair: well-pelted chests, forearms, bellies, butts, and thighs. In other words, I hanker after bears, cubs, and otters. Rarely will the smooth-chested, clean-shaven man arrest my attentions. I love a little brawn, especially well-developed chests and arms, since masculinity is so often equated with strength. I love tattoos, for their suggestions of toughness and wildness, and I love the animality of a little armpit musk. All these butch signifiers I have cultivated over the decades in my own person, which makes me somewhat of a narcissist. I have shaped myself into the sort of man I admire.

Other masculine country-boy signifiers, which I possess in common with my erotic prey? Baseball caps, cowboy hats, camo pants, work boots, and cowboy boots. Wife-beaters, one of the most arousing garments ever, when matched with a hairy chest, a beefy pair of arms, and a little beer belly. Yes, even Southern/mountain accents and manners, country music, and pickup trucks are turn-ons. For me, refinement and urbanity are simply not erotic.

Second, lengthy restraint. Whatever makes a strong man most helpless. Hands tied or cuffed, preferably behind his back. Rope, bondage tape, or duct tape wrapped around his big chest and arms. Ankles bound to prevent his mobility. A gag to silence his speech, a blindfold to seal his sight.

Third, some show of resistance, adding verisimilitude to

kidnapping and abduction fantasies, displaying the captive's strength and requiring disciplinary force on the captor's part. The bottom fights his bonds, shouts into his gag, thrashes about until he has to be held down, roughed up, even threatened with a knife. What would be the thrill, the sense of triumph, in mastering someone who appears weak and entirely willing?

Fourth, some sort of torture, to emphasize the prisoner's vulnerability, his trussed-up inability to escape. Clamps on his nipples. Clothespins lining his pecs, balls, and cock. A paddle, crop, or belt across his ass. Torment leading, with any luck, to butch strength briefly broken down, the delicious extremity of tears.

Fifth, some sort of humiliation, underlining the prisoner's defenselessness, his lack of choice. He's forced to eat from a dog-bowl, to gulp piss, to lap black boots spit-shiny, and to lick spilled cum off the floor. He futilely fights a tight ball-gag till his beard's soaked with drool. Or a rag soaked with piss is stuffed between his teeth and taped securely in.

Sixth, ass-play, from dildos to plugs to initially tender but eventually vigorous ass-fucking. Taking a man, possessing him in his most vulnerable and intimate place, is the rhythmic zenith of any fine leather scene.

Seventh, some sort of tender solicitude, highlighting the captive's dependence, his need to be cared for: spoon-feeding him, cradling him, helping him piss, soothing his hurts, and drying his tears. The powerful made powerless, that sums up this aesthetic. That and, any beautiful butch man is even more beautiful bound and gagged.

I wonder how many others have spent their lives with such a sense of scarcity. My insecurity, shyness, and pride have so often gotten in the way of sexual satisfaction. My stubborn refusal to leave Appalachia and small-town life has as well, reducing considerably the number of butch bottoms I might enjoy. Furthermore, like an oddly large number of leather men, I have ended up in a long-term relationship with a man who is into vanilla sex. John and I share a great deal—we have a fine life together, and I am very lucky to have him—but he does not share my fascination with masculinity in restraint. By now, my age is also a factor; regretfully, if understandably, many of the men I would love to top have no interest in silver-bearded Daddy Bears. These days, Eros is more about fantasy than fact, more about what is achingly imagined than what is sweetly experienced.

Due to all these factors, there have been, over the last thirty years, unfortunately few men I powerfully desired who submitted to me in the ways I wanted. Wistfully, longingly, I remember them.

Steve: with your red mustache, thick, veiny biceps, and snow-pale ass. Here you are again, bandana tied between your teeth, wrists belted together behind your back, grunting beneath me in votive candlelight, loving my cock inside you.

Thomas: my greatest and deepest passion, you who haunt me yet, because our libidos were so perfectly matched; you were such a perfect embodiment of my type—short, muscled, furry—and because our connection lasted for a good while, despite the presence of your carefully deceived husband. And because we both said, "I love you," whatever that meant. I see you still, roped hand and foot, blindfolded and gagged with bandanas, entirely beautiful. I am rocking you in my arms, whispering fervid endearments, stroking the hard, thickly furred mounds of your chest. Together we make a hairy Pietà.

Niles: you bastard, you cover boy. John got to fuck you, I didn't. I still regret that. I remember your hands tied to the headboard, a ball-gag buckled in your mouth, your legs over John's shoulders, getting screwed. So burly, covered with sweat and black hair. Why did you have to be such a shit? Come back, spread your thighs, let me take my turn inside you.

Art: to hell with your jealous, insecure, thoroughly unhot husband. Your submission was so sweet. To have had you only twice maddens me still. God, those nubby nipples, that tight, smooth ass. Bucked and gagged in the basement boiler room, looking up at me with wide eyes, teeth clenching the rubber bit, sighing while I cover you with piss, then leave you to sweat, struggle, and moan in the dark.

And you, black-bearded Zack, chewing the bandana wet while I eat your ass; and you, Tibor, silver-goateed Magyar giant, mouth, wrists, and ankles all taped up, rocking your butt back against my lubed fingers; and you, curly headed Frodo, hands cuffed, eyes and mouth taped, as I drive us through dark mountains from the Roanoke Airport.

Too short a time together, buddies, butch bottoms, hot gentlemen. Evanescent as bloodroot, bluebell, dog's-tooth violet, and other blossoms of an Appalachian spring. I want you all back again.

One of the most arousing, beautiful, and evocative images I've ever encountered I saw first in banner form, plastered over a sex shop on Castro Street a few days before the Folsom Street Fair in 2007. It was an ad for Titan Media's BDSM movie *Fear*: porn star François Sagat, hairy chest crisscrossed with rope, bearded face grimacing with terror, teeth gritted around a rubber bit, thickly muscular arms spread and tied to a two-by-four in a makeshift crucifixion. I could only stand gaping, trying to memorize the sight, muttering stupidly, "Jesus Christ. Jesus Christ." There it was, a perfect embodiment of all my fetishes. And hung over a storefront in broad daylight, for God's sake. Such ads do not appear over storefronts, more's the pity, in my native Appalachia. Studying it, I was reminded of how much my leather aesthetic isolates me from most of humanity.

John bought me the DVD for Christmas that year. I watch it sometimes while I'm on our exercise bike. François struggles and sobs, crying for help against the bit gag as his captors' piss-streams soak him. My response is a mixture of dick-stiff lust, hushed awe, and an almost spiritual reverence, as if a bound and gagged bottom that desirable were a crucified savior or sacrificed god.

At present, until François decides to move to Appalachian Virginia to be my boy; until Joseph and Sam suddenly turn gay and come clamoring my way, begging to be dominated; until sheer luck, coincidence, or my infrequent flirtation on certain bear and leather Internet sites pays off, my hankering for a hairy captive is satisfied only in video, photo, or print, as well as in my own fantasy life, which grows more vivid as I age and as real-life scenarios fade slowly from the realm of probability.

Many are my substitute satisfactions. Here's poor prisoner François getting gang-banged in *Fear*; here's a furry, goateed cub getting tape-gagged in *Hogtied One: Caught at Self-Bondage*. Here are old issues of the sadly now-defunct *Bound & Gagged* magazine; the photo collections *Male Bondage* by Van Darkholme and *13 Years of Bondage* by Rick Castro. Here are fur-pelted, black-bearded, suffering studs restrained with complex Shibari rope-work in Gengoroh Tagame's hot comics, *The House of the Brutes* and *Do You Remember the South Island's P.O.W. Camp*? Here, bound and gagged in various positions in my bed and in my basement dungeon—all, like Joseph and Sam, happily helpless and savoring every submissive second— are several country-music stars and film actors; a few students, past and present; the butcher-boy scruff-cub at Food City; the dark-goateed wonder who put in our storm windows; the hot young guys who painted our bedroom; the lean, stubbly faced country boy who trims our trees. Sooner or later, in imagination or erotic fiction, I will top them all.

Like Kafka's "Hunger Artist," I am most often quietly starving, rarely finding rations that satisfy, but that resultant keen hunger gives me a fiery intensity few I know can match. What I lack in breadth, I gain in obsessive depth and focus. These are gifts, hard-won but true. When I study François' straining, trussed muscles and bit-gagged grimace, I understand the ancient Greeks, who made of their devotion to Eros, Priapus, and Dionysus a kind of religion. Virility, beauty, vulnerability, and suffering—for me, there is no headier mead. I am a hairy hillbilly priest patiently awaiting the next sacrifice, the return of the long-absent god.

About the contributors

DR KEVIN ALDERSON is an associate professor of counseling psychology at the University of Calgary. His areas of research interest include human sexuality, gender studies and gender identity, and gay identity. Throughout his twenty-three years as a psychologist, Dr Alderson has counseled hundreds of sexual minority clients. He is an editor for the *Canadian Journal of Counselling*, a national peer-reviewed professional journal. He writes a monthly column for *Outlooks* magazine and has written for *Gay Calgary & Edmonton Magazine*. His five published books are: *Beyond Coming Out: Experiences of Positive Gay Identity* (Insomniac Press, 2000); *Breaking Out: The Complete Guide to Building and Enhancing a Positive Gay Identity for Men and Women* (Insomniac Press, 2002); *Same-Sex Marriage: The Personal and the Political* (co-authored with Dr. Kathleen Lahey, Insomniac Press, 2004); *Grade Power: The Complete Guide to Improving Your Grades through Self-Hypnosis* (Insomniac Press, 2004); and *"Breathe, Freedom!" Lessons on Kicking the Crap Out of Cigarettes* (self-published, 2007).

PAUL BELLINI was born in Timmins, Ontario, in 1959. After receiving his Bachelor of Arts in Film Studies at York University in 1982, he embarked on a career that includes being a writer on two of Canada's foremost comedy series, *The Kids in the Hall* (1989 to 1995) and *This Hour Has 22 Minutes* (1995 to 1999). Other noteworthy writing assignments include the novel *Buddy Babylon* (Dell, 1998), the theatrical presentation *The Lowest Show on Earth* (2002), and the independent films *Hayseed* (1997) and *doUlike2watch* (2002). He has also worked on various other television shows as both a writer and producer, a career that has garnered three Gemini Awards and three Emmy nominations. He is a columnist for the Toronto-based magazine *fab* and currently lives in Toronto.

STEVEN BEREZNAI is the author of the gay teen superhero novel, *Queeroes* (Jambora Publishing, 2009) and of the "survival guide" *Gay and Single … Forever? 10 Things Every Guy Looking for Love (and Not Finding It) Needs to Know* (Da Capo Press, 2006). He lives in Toronto and can be reached through his website, *stevenbereznai.com*.

S. BEAR BERGMAN (*sbearbergman.com*) is an author, a theater artist, an instigator, a gender-jammer, and a good example of what happens when you overeducate a contrarian. Ze is also the author of *Butch Is a Noun* (Suspect Thoughts Press, 2006), *The Nearest Exit May Be Behind You* (Arsenal Pulp

Press, 2009), and three award-winning solo performance pieces, and ze contributes frequently to anthologies on all manner of topics, from the sacred to the extremely profane. A longtime activist, Bear continues to work at the points of intersection between and among gender, sexuality, and culture, and spends a lot of time keeping people from installing traffic signals there.

'NATHAN BURGOINE's short story "Heart" appears in *Fool for Love: New Gay Fiction* (Cleis Press, 2008), edited by Timothy J. Lambert and R.D. Cochrane. He lives in Ottawa with his husband, Daniel, and can be found on the web at *n8an.livejournal.com*.

TONY CORREIA writes "Queen's Logic" for *Xtra! West* in Vancouver, BC. His essays have appeared in the *Globe and Mail*, the *Vancouver Province*, *subTerrain, Vancouver Review*, and *Second Person Queer* (Arsenal Pulp Press, 2009). For everything Tony Correia, visit *tonycorreia.com*.

DANIEL ALLEN COX is the author of the novel *Shuck* (Arsenal Pulp Press, 2008) and the novella *Tattoo This Madness In* (Dusty Owl Press, 2006). His stories and essays have appeared in the anthologies *Second Person Queer* (Arsenal Pulp Press, 2009) and *Year of the Thief* (Thieves Jargon Press, 2006), as well as in numerous magazines. He writes the column "Fingerprinted" for *Capital Xtra!* and lives in Montreal.

JAMESON CURRIER is the author of the novel *Where the Rainbow Ends* (Overlook Press, 2000) and three collections of short stories: *Dancing on the Moon* (Penguin Books, 1994), *Desire, Lust, Passion, Sex* (Green Candy Press, 2004), and *Still Dancing* (Lethe Press, 2008).

MARTIN DELACROIX writes novels, novellas, and short fiction. He lives on Florida's Gulf Coast.

LEWIS DESIMONE is the author of the novel *Chemistry* (Lethe Press, 2008). His work has also appeared in *Christopher Street, James White Review, Harrington Gay Men's Fiction Quarterly*, and the anthologies *Beyond Definition: New Writing from Gay and Lesbian San Francisco* (Manic D Press, 1994), *Charmed Lives: Gay Spirit in Storytelling* (White Crane Books, 2006), *Best Gay Love Stories: Summer Flings* (Alyson Books, 2007), *My Diva: 65 Gay Men on the Women Who Inspire Them* (Terrace Books, 2009), and *Second Person Queer* (Arsenal Pulp Press, 2009). He blogs regularly at *sexandthesissy.wordpress.com*. A native Bostonian, he lives in San Francisco, where he is working on his second novel. He can be reached through *lewisdesimone.com*.

VIET DINH was born in Đà Lạt, Vietnam, in 1974 and spent his formative years in Aurora, Colorado. He received his MFA from the University of Houston and currently lives in Wilmington, Delaware. In 2008, he received a fiction fellowship from the National Endowment for the Arts. His work has appeared in *The PEN/O. Henry Prize Stories 2009* (Anchor Books, 2009), *Zoetrope: All-Story*, *Threepenny Review*, *Five Points*, *Fence*, and *Michigan Quarterly Review*, among others.

CHRISTOPHER DIRADDO is a Montreal-based writer and publicist. His short stories have appeared in *Quickies 3* (Arsenal Pulp Press, 2003) and the Lambda Award-winning *First Person Queer* (Arsenal Pulp Press, 2007). He is working on his first novel and can be contacted at *christopherdiraddo.com*.

LANDON DIXON's credits include stories in the magazines *In Touch*, *Indulge*, *Three Pillows*, *Men*, *Freshmen*, *[2]*, *Mandate*, *Torso*, and *Honcho*; and in the anthologies *Straight? Vol. 2* (Alyson Books, 2003), *Friction 7* (Alyson Books, 2004), *Working Stiff* (Alyson Books, 2006), *Sex by the Book* (Green Candy Press, 2007), *Ultimate Gay Erotica 2005, 2007*, and *2008* (Alyson Books), and *Best Gay Erotica 2009* (Cleis Press, 2008).

LARRY DUPLECHAN is the author of five acclaimed gay-themed novels, including *Blackbird* (Little Sister's Classics/Arsenal Pulp Press, 2006) and the Lambda Literary Award-winning *Got 'til It's Gone* (Arsenal Pulp Press, 2008).

DANIEL GAWTHROP is the author of *The Rice Queen Diaries: A Memoir* (Arsenal Pulp Press, 2005), *Affirmation: The AIDS Odyssey of Dr Peter* (New Star Press, 1994), and two other works of nonfiction. His essay "Marriage: Why I Took the Plunge" was published in *First Person Queer* (Arsenal Pulp Press, 2007).

SKY GILBERT is a writer, director, and drag queen extraordinaire. He was co-founder and artistic director of Buddies in Bad Times Theatre (North America's largest gay and lesbian theater) for eighteen years. He is the author of the novels *Guilty* (Insomniac Press, 1998), *St. Stephen's* (Insomniac Press, 1999) and *I Am Kasper Klotz* (ECW Press, 2001), the theater memoir *Ejaculations from the Charm Factory* (ECW Press, 2000), and two poetry collections, *Digressions of a Naked Party Girl* (ECW Press, 1998) and *Temptations for a Juvenile Delinquent* (ECW Press, 2003). He has received two Dora Mavor Moore Awards and the Pauline McGibbon Award for theater directing, and he was recently the recipient of the Margo Bindhardt Award (from the Toronto Arts Foundation), the Silver Ticket Award (from the Toronto

Alliance for the Performing Arts), and the ReLit Award for his fourth novel, *An English Gentleman* (Cormorant Books, 2004). He also recently received a PhD from the University of Toronto. Sky had two books published in 2007: the novel *Brother Dumb* (ECW Press) and the play *Bad Acting Teachers* (Playwrights Canada Press). Sky holds a University Research Chair in Creative Writing and Theatre Studies at the School of English and Theatre Studies at Guelph University.

JUSTIN HALL loves comic books, and he especially loves comics about sex and travel. Best known for *True Travel Tales*, his comic book series of true-life adventures from the road, Hall has also been featured in numerous other publications, such as *Best American Comics* (Houghton Mifflin, 2006), *Best Erotic Comics* (Last Gasp, 2008/2009), and *Boy Trouble* (Green Candy Press, 2006/2008), as well as in various museum and gallery shows. Hall produces the gay porn comic *Hard to Swallow* with fellow pervert Dave Davenport, as well as the adventures of *Glamazonia the Uncanny Super Tranny*. You can check out his work at *allthumbspress.com* and his porn comics at *hardtoswallowcomics.com*.

AARON HAMBURGER was awarded the Rome Prize by the American Academy of Arts and Letters for his short story collection, *The View from Stalin's Head* (Random House, 2004), also nominated for a Violet Quill Award. His next book, a novel titled *Faith for Beginners* (Random House, 2005), was nominated for a Lambda Literary Award. His writing has appeared in *Poets and Writers*, *Tin House*, *Details*, and *Out*. He has received fellowships from the Edward F. Albee Foundation and the Civitella Ranieri Foundation in Umbria, Italy, and he teaches creative writing at Columbia University.

MARK AMBROSE HARRIS has lived in Montreal all of his queer life. When he was in Grade Six, the other boys wanted to be hockey players, but Mark wanted to be Annie Lennox. His work is often concerned with the intersections of queer identity, sound, sexuality, and music. However, he is also interested in spiders, sharks, and cephalopods. He writes, sings, plays keys, and performs with the band On Bodies. His writing has appeared in *Lickety Split*, *Intersections/Canadian University Music Review*, and *Outsider Ink*. In 2008, his sound installation, "Pornographic Gender," was featured in interAural, a group show at the Room and Board Gallery. In the winter of 2007, he began the Sound Sex Project, an ongoing archival work, which can be accessed at *soundsexproject.blogspot.com*. He completed his MA thesis, *My Body is a Mix Tape: Music and Desire in the Sound Sex Project*, in the Media Studies program at Concordia University in 2008. The stegosaurus is his favorite dinosaur.

WAYNE HOFFMAN is the author of *Hard: A Novel* (Carroll & Graf, 2006), and screenwriter of the short film *Sucker*, based on the novel. His fiction has appeared in *Velvet Mafia*, the *Forward*, and *Harrington Gay Men's Literary Quarterly*. He has also published essays in numerous anthologies, including *Boy Meets Boy* (St. Martin's, 1999), *Bar Stories* (Alyson Books, 2000), *Mama's Boy* (Painted Leaf, 2000), *Generation Q* (Alyson Books, 1996), and *Men Seeking Men* (Painted Leaf, 1998). As a journalist, he has written for everyone from the *Washington Post* and the *Nation* to *Torso* and *Unzipped*. He lives in New York City, where he inspects men's briefs on a regular basis.

SHAUN LEVIN is the author of *A Year of Two Summers* (Five Leaves, 2005) and *Seven Sweet Things* (bluechrome, 2003). His most recent work is *Isaac Rosenberg's Journey to Arras: A Meditation* (Cecil Woolf, 2008). His stories appear in anthologies as diverse as *Between Men* (Running Press, 2007), *Modern South African Stories* (Ad Donker, 2003), *Boyfriends from Hell* (Green Candy Press, 2003), several editions of *Best Gay Erotica* (Cleis Press), and *The Slow Mirror: New Fiction by Jewish Writers* (Five Leaves, 2008). He is the editor of *Chroma: A Queer Literary Journal*. See more at *shaunlevin.com* and *chroma-journal.co.uk*.

K.P. LUKOFF is a twenty-five-year-old Brooklynite, making ends meet by working in a bookstore and establishing a career as a writer.

STEVE MacISAAC: Too contemplative to be porno and too explicit to be anything else, the three issues released to date of MacIsaac's *Shirtlifter* all examine the intersection of sexuality, personality, and society. *Sticky*, his collaboration with Dale Lazarov, was released by Bruno Gmünder in 2006. Current work in progress can be seen three days a week at *moderntales.com* or at his website, *stevemacisaac.com*.

JEFF MANN grew up in Covington, Virginia, and Hinton, West Virginia, receiving degrees in English and forestry from West Virginia University. His poetry, fiction, and essays have appeared in the *Spoon River Poetry Review*, *Wild Sweet Notes: Fifty Years of West Virginia Poetry 1950-1999*, *Prairie Schooner*, *Shenandoah*, *Laurel Review*, the *Gay and Lesbian Review Worldwide*, *Crab Orchard Review*, *West Branch*, *Bloom*, *Appalachian Heritage*, several editions of *Best Gay Erotica* (Cleis Press), *Best Gay Poetry 2008* (A Midsummer's Night Press/Lethe Press 2008), and *Best Gay Stories 2008* (Lethe Press, 2008). He has published three award-winning poetry chapbooks, *Bliss* (Brich House Books, 1998), *Mountain Fireflies* (Poetic Matrix Press, 2000), and *Flint Shards from Sussex* (Gival Press, 2000); two full-length books of poetry, *Bones Washed with Wine* (Gival Press, 2003) and *On the Tongue* (Gival Press,

2006); a collection of personal essays, *Edge: Travels of an Appalachian Leather Bear* (Harrington Park Press, 2003/Bear Bones Books, 2008); a novella, "Devoured," included in *Masters of Midnight: Erotic Tales of the Vampire* (Kensington Books, 2003); a book of poetry and memoir, *Loving Mountains, Loving Men* (Ohio University Press, 2005); and a volume of short fiction, *A History of Barbed Wire* (Suspect Thoughts Press, 2006), which won a Lambda Literary Award. He teaches creative writing at Virginia Tech in Blacksburg, Virginia.

TIM MILLER's solo performances, hailed for their humor and passion, have delighted and emboldened audiences all over the world. He is the author of *Shirts & Skins* (Alyson Books, 1997), *Body Blows* (University of Wisconsin Press, 2002), and *1001 Beds* (Terrace Books, 2006). Check out *timmillerperformer.com*.

JAY NEAL is a long-time connoisseur of beards and aficionado of men with body hair. He wouldn't have minded a more exciting sexual history, but his suburban neuroticism has provided material for lots of stories. His fiction has appeared in several magazines and about twenty anthologies. He and his bear partner share a life of domestic contentment in suburban Washington, DC.

ANDY QUAN, Canadian-born and Sydney-based, is the author of four books: *Six Positions* (Green Candy Press, 2006); a short story collection, *Calendar Boy* (New Star Books, 2001); and two poetry collections, *Slant* (Nightwood Editions, 2001) and *Bowling Pin Fire* (Signature Editions, 2007). His work has appeared in many anthologies of gay fiction and erotica in North America, Australia, and Europe. He's obsessed with succulents, is reviving the art of the mix-tape in CD form, practices reiki, sings songs, and occasionally updates his website at *andyquan.com*.

JEFFREY ROTIN is a freelance writer, magazine editor, and consultant to nonprofits. His nonfiction work has appeared in *First Person Queer* (Arsenal Pulp Press, 2007), the *LOOP*, and on the *Early Edition* and *Outfront* on CBC Radio One. Born and raised in Toronto, he lives in Vancouver.

DON SHEWEY has published three books about theater and written articles for many publications, including the *New York Times*, the *Village Voice*, *Esquire*, and *Rolling Stone*. His erotic writing has been anthologized in numerous anthologies, including *Bears* (Cleis Press, 2008), *The Mammoth Book of Gay Erotica* (Carroll & Graf, 1997), *Best of the Best Gay Erotica* (Cleis Press, 2000), *Male Lust* (Routledge, 2000), *Boyfriends from Hell* (Green

Candy Press, 2003), and *Sex by the Book* (Green Candy Press, 2007). His 1991 "X-rated" interview with Madonna for the *Advocate* was syndicated around the world to nineteen countries in eleven languages. He grew up in a trailer park on a dirt road in Waco, Texas, and lives in midtown Manhattan halfway between Trump Tower and Carnegie Hall. An archive of his writing can be found online at *donshewey.com*.

JAY STARRE, a resident of Vancouver, has written for numerous gay men's magazines, including *Torso* and *Men*. His torrid stories have also been included in almost fifty anthologies, among them *Quickies 3* (Arsenal Pulp Press, 2003) and *Bears* (Cleis Press, 2008). He's the author of a steamy historical novel, *The Erotic Tales of the Knights Templars in the Holy Land* (StarBooks, 2007); *The Lusty Adventures of the Knossos Prince* is forthcoming.

SHAWN SYMS has been writing about sexuality for twenty years. His work appears in *First Person Queer* (Arsenal Pulp Press, 2007) and a couple of dozen other publications.

ZACHARY TAYLOR, in addition to reclaiming his "other" erotic biography, writes scripts and produces videos for human rights and other advocacy groups. "Choice Cuts" is his first published essay.

JERRY L. WHEELER's work has appeared in *Law of Desire: Tales of Gay Male Lust and Obsession* (Alyson Books, 2004), *Focus on the Fabulous: Colorado GLBT Voices* (Johnson Books, 2007), and *I Do! An Anthology in Support of Marriage Equality* (MLR Press, 2008), and online, in *Velvet Mafia*. Stuck in the ninth circle of first-novel hell (*The Dead Book*), he continues slogging to the far shore of the Lake of Fire in asbestos waders.

ROB WOLFSHAM is a twenty-two-year-old recent college graduate living in Lubbock, Texas. He enjoys writing about homomasculinity and instances where Jesus cockblocks him … or doesn't. Among his vices are CSPAN, political blogs, army fatigues, and burly redheads. He contributes a column to *nightcharm.com*, and his first published story was in *Boy Crazy* (Cleis Press, 2009), edited by Richard Labonté. Read his musings at *wolfshammy.com*.

About the editors

RICHARD LABONTÉ has edited almost thirty erotic anthologies for Cleis Press, including the thrice-nominated, twice-Lambda Literary Award-winning Best Gay Erotica series; coedited (with Lawrence Schimel) *The Future is Queer*, *First Person Queer* (also a Lammy winner), and *Second Person Queer* for Arsenal Pulp Press; writes a fortnightly book review column for Q Syndicate; reviews contemporary fiction, gay nonfiction, and books about the environment for *Publishers Weekly*; and transmutes turgid technical writing into bright golden prose for assorted clients. In part one of his post-university life, he wrote and edited for the *Citizen* newspaper in Ottawa, Ontario; in part two, he helped found and eventually managed A Different Light Bookstores in Los Angeles, West Hollywood, San Francisco, and New York; in part three—since returning to Canada in 2001—he has been self-employed as a freelance editor and reviewer. He lives on Bowen Island, British Columbia, with his husband, Asa Liles, and four-footed companions Zak and Tiger-Lily.

LAWRENCE SCHIMEL is a full-time author and anthologist who has published more than ninety books, including three previous anthologies coedited with Richard Labonté for Arsenal Pulp Press: *First Person Queer* (2007), *Second Person Queer* (2009), and *The Future is Queer* (2006). Some of his other titles include *Best Gay Poetry 2008* (A Midsummer Night's Press/Lethe Press, 2008), *Best Date Ever* (Alyson, 2007), *Two Boys in Love* (Seventh Window, 2006), *The Drag Queen of Elfland* (Circlet, 1997), *The Mammoth Book of New Gay Erotica* (Carroll & Graf, 2007), and *Fairy Tales for Writers* (A Midsummer Night's Press, 2007). Writing in Spanish, his books include the poetry collection *Desayuno en la cama* (Desatada/Egales, 2008), the graphic novel *Vacaciones en Ibiza* (Egales, 2003), and the children's books *Amigos y vecinos* (Ediciones La Librería, 2005), *La aventura de Cecilia y el dragón* (Bibliópolis, 2005), and *Cosas que puedo hacer yo solo* (Macmillan, 2007), among others. *First Person Queer* won a Lambda Literary Award in 2008, and *PoMoSexuals* (Cleis Press, 1997), coedited with Carol Queen, won in 1998; he has been a finalist for the award eleven other times. His writings have been translated into Basque, Catalan, Croatian, Czech, Dutch, Esperanto, Finnish, French, Galician, German, Greek, Hungarian, Icelandic, Indonesian, Italian, Japanese, Polish, Portuguese, Romanian, Russian, Serbian, Slovene, Slovak, and Spanish.